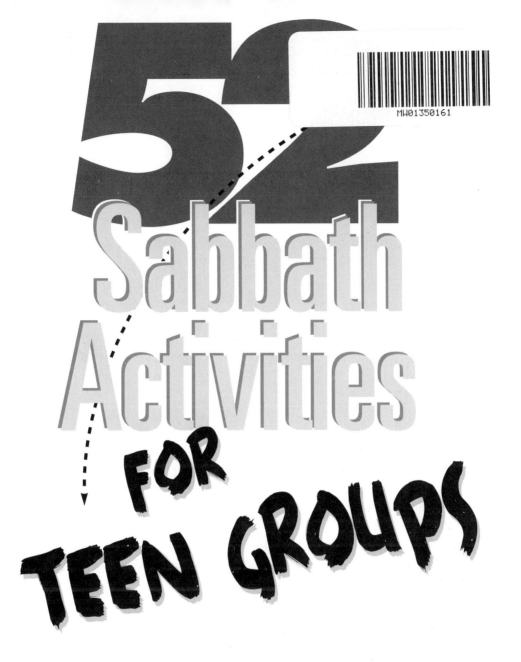

52 Sabbath Activities for Teen Groups

A Resource of Proven, Surefire, Guaranteed-fun Activities That Make Sabbaths Unforgettable for Youth

Don Pate

REVIEW AND HERALD® PUBLISHING ASSOCIATION
HAGERSTOWN, MD 21740

Copyright © 1995 by
Review and Herald® Publishing Association

The author assumes full responsibility for the accuracy of all facts and quotations as cited in this book.

This book was
Edited by Richard W. Coffen
Interior design by Patricia S. Wegh
Cover design by Mark O'Connor
Cover photos by Ripple, © 1994 Nicholas DeSciose
           Bee, © L. Fritz/H. Armstrong Roberts
Typeset: 12/16 Futura Book

PRINTED IN U.S.A.

02 01 00   5 4 3 2

R&H Cataloging Service
Pate, Don, 1951-
    52 Sabbath activities for teen groups: a resource of proven, surefire guaranteed-fun activities that make Sabbaths unforgettable for youth.

    1. Sabbath keeping. 2. Youth-Religious life. 3. Students, Seventh-day Adventist—Religious life. 4. Youth leadership. I. Title.

        263.2

ISBN 0-8280-0941-4

Dedication

Certain people have become exceedingly precious to me through recent events in my life. . . . Don and Marolyn Wagner, Gemmie and Blanche Baker, Ed and Judy Rosaasen, Alan and Lynette Newhart, Richard Parrish, Darlene Smith, and Al Ells to mention a few.

I do owe Ken Hutchins particular thanks for his hours of efforts on my behalf. (Not everyone will stick his or her neck out for another as you have.)

But there are two men whom I must express special appreciation to. If all denominational leaders had the redemptive spirits exhibited by these men, we would be a church singularly blessed.

Larry Caviness

About eight years ago you told me that I needed a job that would just allow me to create and create for our church. My friend, this attempt is a bit of that. I hope this book rewards you, even if only fractionally, for what I owe you.

Herman Bauman

For years you have been a proponent of grace. I know, to my core, that grace is not just talk with you. I'll never forget what you have done for me . . . truly amazing grace! This book, and so much more, is for you.

Baruch atah Adonai, Eloheinu Melech ha-olam,
shenatan m-cheno l-bashar v-adam.

Contents

Introduction

Part 1   **A Little Background**
Chapter 1   My Only Touch of Divinity ➤ **9**
Chapter 2   I Don't Want to Keep the Sabbath Anymore ➤ **13**
Chapter 3   Sabbath Was Never
                     Supposed to Be an Accident! ➤ **19**

Part 2   **Sabbath Activities**
Activity 1   Adopt a Student Missionary ➤ **22**
Activity 2   Quadrant Art ➤ **24**
Activity 3   Bible Sand Sculpture Contest ➤ **26**
Activity 4   Cake Art ➤ **28**
Activity 5   Reminiscent Therapy ➤ **30**
Activity 6   Play Dough Idols ➤ **32**
Activity 7   The Guilt Backpack ➤ **34**
Activity 8   The *Jerusalem Observer* ➤ **36**
Activity 9   The Great Family Switch ➤ **38**
Activity 10   Musical Balloons ➤ **40**
Activity 11   Exposing the Great Lie ➤ **42**
Activity 12   Sukkah Hopping ➤ **44**
Activity 13   Dual Jeopardy ➤ **46**
Activity 14   The Forum ➤ **48**
Activity 15   Young Mother's Lifelines ➤ **50**
Activity 16   The Observant Communion ➤ **52**
Activity 17   Making a Mezuzah ➤ **54**
Activity 18   Window Murals ➤ **56**

Activity 19	The Great "Love" Mixer ➤ **58**	
Activity 20	Scripture Acrostics Game ➤ **60**	
Activity 21	The Welcome Pack ➤ **62**	
Activity 22	The Midrash Walk ➤ **64**	
Activity 23	The *Shekel Shopper* ➤ **66**	
Activity 24	City Planners ➤ **68**	
Activity 25	The Great Prophecy Clip ➤ **70**	
Activity 26	Performing Tashlick ➤ **72**	
Activity 27	Bible Boggle ➤ **74**	
Activity 28	Aunt Tillie's Gift ➤ **76**	
Activity 29	Creation Texture Boxes ➤ **78**	
Activity 30	The Heritage Video ➤ **80**	
Activity 31	Bible Baseball ➤ **82**	
Activity 32	The Hezekiah Tree ➤ **84**	
Activity 33	The Revelation Relief ➤ **86**	
Activity 34	Bible Actionary ➤ **88**	
Activity 35	*Challah* and Love Loaves ➤ **90**	
Activity 36	Sand Painting ➤ **92**	
Activity 37	The Conflict Mirror ➤ **94**	
Activity 38	The Sabbath Crest ➤ **96**	
Activity 39	Bible May I? ➤ **98**	
Activity 40	The "What If?" Challenge ➤ **100**	
Activity 41	The Lord's Prayer Hunt ➤ **102**	
Activity 42	The Language of Heaven ➤ **104**	
Activity 43	The Jerusalem Miniature ➤ **106**	
Activity 44	The Adam and Eve Walk ➤ **108**	
Activity 45	The Christmas Jewels ➤ **110**	
Activity 46	Living Psalms ➤ **112**	
Activity 47	Muddy Fingernails ➤ **114**	
Activity 48	The Family Courtroom ➤ **116**	
Activity 49	Parables Now ➤ **118**	
Activity 50	The Ministry Cycle ➤ **120**	
Activity 51	Sabbath Monuments ➤ **122**	
Activity 52	Kingdom Reunions ➤ **124**	

Introduction

During my 20 years of professional service to the Seventh-day Adventist Church, I've filled the roles of (1) seventh-grade teacher in Tennessee, (2) boys' dean as well as religion and history teacher in New Mexico, (3) teacher of grades 3 through 8 in Texas, (4) pastor in Michigan and California, (5) academy chaplain in Texas, and (6) campus pastor and Bible teacher in Arizona.

Additionally, I've had the blessed privilege of speaking at many camp meetings, seminars, youth rallies, summer camps, and retreats in 22 North American Division conferences and on four other continents.

That variety of experience guaranteed two things: (1) someday I was going to figure out what I was supposed to be, and (2) I was responsible for a lot of Sabbath activities during those years.

Nearly all the hands-on activities included in this book are of my own creation, but even those have been shaped by many of the people who have contributed richly to my Sabbaths throughout the years. I'd certainly like to give full credit and thanks by name to those whose ideas I've adapted for this book, but I don't even know where to begin. I am grateful for these creative people, and they should be honored for their efforts and creativity.

I also wish to thank Des Cummings, Jr., for sparking my mind back in 1979 with the concept that most Sabbathkeepers regard Sabbath as an evolutionary act. One sentence from a sermon of his was the catalyst for a great deal of my thinking in this regard during the intervening years. Chapter 3 expands on that thought.

I pray that this book will serve as a useful tool for enriching the Sabbath experience of many. I urge you to use, perfect, and adapt anything you wish from this book. Shape the events to your own circum-

stances, and make them better than I could have. The concept of copyright is merely a legal necessity. This is a book to be used. I wish only to provide a springboard for your greater creativity.
    Enjoy!

**Part 1
A Little Background**

Chapter One

My Only Touch of Divinity

How can you describe the quantum theory to a 4-year-old? (For that matter, how are you to describe it to me?)

➤ How do you verbalize the gradations of burning color in a glorious desert sunset to a person who has been blind from birth?

➤ Try to sit your friendly parakeet down and get it to understand why its chores for this week include doing the dishes . . . and how it is to do them in the fashion that pleases your picky mother-in-law.

➤ Explain the *beged kefet* rule of Hebrew grammar to your cat.

➤ Put yourself in Peter's sandals and explain nuclear holocaust with a term other than "the elements shall melt with fervent heat" (2 Peter 3:12).

➤ Teach your goldfish how to shoot a wrist shot at an empty hockey net.

The problem with these scenarios is that you're dealing with dual limitations. Not only are the "receptors" of the message limited in their scope of understanding (that is, the child, the parakeet, the cat, etc.), but also the "transmitters" of the message are limited by their own knowledge and language capabilities.

Even if you could find a cat who just might have a passing interest in Hebrew, you'd likely be stuck because of your own lack of abilities, the limitation of your knowledge of the subject, and your capability to verbalize it in a way the cat could understand.

52 Sabbath Activities for Teen Groups

Dual limitation renders the scenario hopeless.

But what if you were Wayne Gretzky and therefore stood as the undisputed greatest hockey player of all time? Would you not be the lone recognized authority on how to shoot a wrist shot at an empty net? In that scenario you'd be dealing with only the limitations placed upon the situation by the incapacity of the goldfish, which would still be insurmountable. (My 2-year-old niece could stop any wrist shot from your goldfish; they're notoriously bad skaters and have some of the weakest wrists in the league.)

You're probably asking yourself, "Where in the world is he going with this stuff?" I'm seeking to explain why I can't explain God. More than that, this whole concept of limitations explains why even God can't explain God—at least to you and me.

The Bible declares that God has no limitations, but the problem is that you and I do. Even though God can do everything perfectly, our lack of capacity limits His limitless abilities. He can do it all, I just don't have the "wrists" for it. That's why we struggle with what the theologians have called "the ultimate Other" or "the Ineffable" or "the Transcendent."

God is limited, but limited by *my* capacity. The ocean cannot be held in a four-ounce baby bottle with holes in it. Therefore, I'm stuck with understanding only facets of God. I cannot comprehend the full picture, so I'm allowed to look dimly at just tiny pieces and trust the small portion of the picture that I can *begin* to comprehend.

Exactly what aspects of God does the Bible tell us? It either states outright or implies that He is, among other things, omniscient (fully knowing), omnipresent (without restriction of time or space), and omnipotent (all-powerful). Accordingly, God is unhampered by our limitations in what He knows, where He is, and what He can do.

Little wonder that David Seamands, of Asbury Seminary, once looked at me and said, "Don, one of these days you young guys have to learn there are no vacancies in the Trinity."

There are so many things I don't know, and at times I chomp at the bit because of that limitation. I'm restricted by time and space, and that's frustrating to no end.

I'd love to be in Jerusalem today. (I'd love to be in Jerusalem *any* day.) I'd give almost anything to go back to various times of my life to undo some of what I've done, but all the wishing in the world doesn't seem to bring that to pass. I dream of adjusting my future so that I could sit with you and share this material (and have you teach me in return) rather than let you merely read it. But the reality is that I'm sitting in my here and now and have no power over past or future, no matter how hard I hold my breath.

My Only Touch of Divinity

I covet the ability to make things happen. I often find myself putting my hands into the works, trying to force the outcome in certain situations or attempting to change other people's attitudes and actions. I usually find only disappointment in my efforts. Rarely can I effect anything by my will. There are so many ways in life that I'm impotent.

I'm figuring out—gradually, I fear—that I am not God. And the fact that I'm only beginning to figure out that I'm not God proves again that I am not. If I were God, I wouldn't have to figure anything out.

So despite what every New Age woo-woo this side of Sedona says, it appears that I'm not God. I'm not one with the universe. Dolphins are not my brothers, and I'm only a small piece of the whole.

Adam may have borne God's image, but that did not make him God any more than the fake computer shells decorating office supply stores would be able to crunch out the information I'm putting onto the screen of my trusty old Mac-plus here. Apologies to the old ad campaign of Andre Agassi, but the reality is that although perception may be something, image is nothing.

> **I covet the ability to make things happen. I often find myself putting my hands into the works.**

The portions of divinity in my makeup do not make me God any more than my dog's toenails render him fit to sit at the supper table with the rest of the family.

My cellular base is carbon, and so is that of the palm tree in front of my window here. I'm not a palm tree, and it's not writing this book. Fractions of similarities don't make equals.

I do have some knowledge, but it's pathetically limited. I do control the present to some degree and can make choices to affect the future, but I'm not omnipresent. I do make some things happen, but there's a world of things that I have no power over at all.

So if God is omniscient, omnipresent, and omnipotent and I am not, then what do I have that might be one drop of divinity?

Creativity!

Creativity is the one facet of God that seemed to be passed on through the kiss of life by the side of the garden river that Friday in Eden. No other part of the creation had that intimate privilege. Mountains and waterfalls were called into existence. Constellations and tulips were spoken into being. But Adam (whose Hebrew name denotes humanity) was created in the image of the Creator. That made him something more. It gave him the position of dominion.

52 Sabbath Activities for Teen Groups

Spiders spin delicate webs, but we call the action "instinct." Instinct brings about the flight paths of geese and the homing nature of salmon and the nesting urge of ospreys. Instinct also causes my dog to sniff every disgusting mark on the passenger list of the telephone pole, when he could be admiring the scenery.

Instinct requires no advance preparation. It just comes about by urge. Instinct doesn't allow for adaptation when the climate or environment changes without warning. It just does what the preprogramming requires. Instinct never put air-conditioning in the barn in the summer.

Creation requires planning and design. Of all creation humans alone carry the ability of creativity. It is the one facet of divinity that I—and you—can rightfully claim.

And if God truly created my gift of creativity, then it must be part of His plan and not just a curious evolutionary development that sets me apart from those creatures with wings and fins and hooves.

Therefore, if we wish to exercise the only aspect of God that makes us somewhat more "divine" than our four-footed friends, we must strive for greater creativity. But the dilemma comes with time pressures. How are we to increase that one facet of divinity in our lives when so much of life is based upon reaction, nuts-and-bolts necessities, and the demands of schedule? Wouldn't it appear that a truly all-knowing, all-powerful Creator would come up with something to allow us time to stretch the one aspect that makes us like Him?

He has! It's called Sabbath, and that's what this book is about—a hands-on guide to challenge your creativity in the realm that God ordained you'd be able.

I dream that this book will be a springboard for greater Sabbath creativity than I have ever known myself. I pray that many will be inspired by this beginning and that soon I'll be able to borrow from some of your rich creativity too!

If we could live this experience, I feel that we'd know what it means to bask in God's happy smile. So dig in. Let your creative juices be primed. Find an experience that is waiting at the end of your labors. Be like God!

Chapter Two

I Don't Want to Keep the Sabbath Anymore

When Jesus didn't quite fit into the box demanded by the religious structure of His day, He was criticized. This censure generally revolved around ritual understandings and expectations.
He was told that

➤ He didn't have the proper credentials for rabbinic teaching, and therefore He didn't perform the ritual cleansing ceremonies to their satisfaction.

➤ His mingling with every Tom, Dick, and harlot was not appropriate.

➤ His respect for their established lines of authority was in question.

➤ His followers were an embarrassment and threat to the structure.

➤ His Sabbath observance was not acceptable.

In responding to that last challenge, Jesus said: "The sabbath was made for man" (Mark 2:27).
God looked at the creature of His hand, and knew that he—we—needed one day to tap back into the Source. He knew that we'd never stay centered well without a special reminder of who was God around here and who wasn't. He knew that a special enhancement to life would come through this divine appointment.

52 Sabbath Activities for Teen Groups

Even before the isolation and lostness of sin, God knew that Adam (read "humanity") needed the texture and flavor that Sabbath would provide to life. What, then, should Sabbath be to those of us who have never been anywhere near Eden?

We've tried to shape Sabbath into many things, and almost universally that has brought about limitation to the day. We try to "keep" the Sabbath. To keep something implies that we've put boundaries and walls around it so that it can't escape. If we want to keep something, we bind it up so that we can control it.

To my way of thinking, "keeping Sabbath" diminishes the day, and that's exactly the opposite of the implications of what creativity is all about. To keep Sabbath is completely contrary to the idea of having that time stand as a memorial to Creation. And that becomes especially true if you've been told that you've been punished because you didn't keep it well.

For generations faithful prophets had warned the people of Judah that if they didn't get their act together in the covenant, they were going to pay. To this day observant Jews hold Tishah b'Ab (the ninth day of the month of Ab) as a commemoration and memorial, because on that day both Temples were destroyed in Israel's history. The Babylonians overran the city and desecrated Solomon's Temple on that day, and on the anniversary 600 years later the Romans torched Herod's Temple. Why did those calamities take place? The prophets said it was because of disobedience.

We Christians often find ourselves criticizing the Pharisees for their exactions and extrapolations of law, but what we don't realize is that the development of the Pharisaic movement and mentality was a completely natural and logical response to the Babylonian captivity and later Roman domination.

If you've been told that you've been punished for disobedience, then it might seem logical to make sure that you're never caught disobeying again. You'd multiply restrictions to make sure that you wouldn't cross any of the forbidden lines at all.

This simple truth can be seen in a parable. Let's suppose that when you first got your driver's license you exceeded the posted speed limit one time. When the police officer pulled you over, he didn't just write you a citation but also took you outside the car and beat you to a bloody pulp. As he scraped your remains off the road and dumped you back in your seat, he admonished you, "Remember, this happens to everyone in the car anytime you exceed the speed limit."

Ten years later you're driving along with your beloved spouse and two small children when you see a police officer by the side of the road.

I Don't Want to Keep the Sabbath Anymore

In horror, you glance down and discover that you've slipped over the speed limit. As you pray desperately that he hasn't noticed your car, you begin to count your options as to how you're going to guarantee that this will never happen again.

For the sake of your precious children you might install a governor on your car that cuts in 10 miles an hour *below* the speed limit, because you'd never want to risk even edging close to the danger zone. You might also install an electric warning system hooked up to your speedometer so that sirens and bells would scream and wail at eight miles below the limit—just in case your governor failed.

But what if you had a double system failure? What if you were going down a steep hill and your foot was completely off the accelerator? What if your car was red, and it carried only the perception that it was going faster? What if the radar gun was defective?

Eventually you'd walk.

If you have enough limitations defined, then you can guarantee that you'll never be caught disobedient.

Now do you understand why people who are afraid to break rules will multiply rules? If you have enough limitations defined, then you can guarantee that you'll never be caught disobedient. If ignorance is no excuse, then you'd better make sure that you're not ignorant.

Pharisees gradually defined more and more rules, because they didn't want ever to be accused of being disobedient again. One trip to Babylon was enough.

Imagine the rabbis' dilemma when the Temple was destroyed the second time. Here they had spent hundreds of years of cautious religious practice so that they could avoid anything that might even appear to be sin, and they got slapped again. Out of that dilemma developed the extrapolations of the Mishnah. Every potential facet of every law and expectation became codified and enhanced. Every possible argument and implication of the law was written down.

That's why the tractate "Shabbat" has 39 categories of prohibitions regarding the Sabbath. It makes for very curious reading—pages and pages of such things as

➤ You can't swim on the Sabbath, because you might break the agricultural prohibition. (As you come up out of the water your robe might accidentally drip on a blade of grass, irrigating it.)

52 Sabbath Activities for Teen Groups

➤ You can't drag a chair across the floor on Sabbath, because it also risks crossing the agricultural prohibition. (You might create a furrow in the earthen floor of your house into which a seed might accidentally fall.)

➤ You can't write more than one Hebrew letter on Sabbath. (There are no words in Hebrew of only one letter; if you were to write two letters, you might make a word.)

And it goes on and on.
But remember, if you can be so very careful and stay at four miles an hour, you don't have to worry about the police dragging you out of your car and beating you senseless. Unless, of course, you're stopped for impeding traffic and thus endangering lives.

I well remember the Friday evening I spent in a "Learning Shabbat" activity at the Hillel Center of Lerhaus Judaica. An imminent rabbi was going to assist some of the *Baalim Teshuvah* (secular Jews returning to ways of observance—backsliders coming home) in learning appropriate Sabbath issues.

With about 70 Jews he was sharing some of the modern dilemmas (such as making sure that you take the light bulb out of your refrigerator so that you don't light a lamp on the Sabbath when you open the door, because that breaks the prohibition against lighting a fire).

I was the only Gentile in the room. After nearly two hours a little white-haired lady on the front row spoke up and said, "Reb, how is this to be called a day of rest? If you have to worry every moment about every little action, how could you ever rest?"

Out of the mouths of babes and grandmothers . . . What insight!

"Keeping Sabbath" is anathema. Restricting the day and limiting its potential by multiplied extrapolations only guarantees that the day will be a burden. And Jews aren't alone in this. One of the understood but unwritten laws regarding Sabbath in the area where I grew up was that you couldn't take photographs on Sabbath unless it was a picture you couldn't take at any other time. We all knew the rule was there in Hezekiah 4:31 or somewhere.

We also weren't to swim on Sabbath. One of the best challenges I heard on this was the story of a dear friend. He had served as a missionary in East Africa, and one weekend there was a large convocation at a camp on the Indian Ocean coast.

The Sabbath morning had been rich, and as the afternoon drew on my friend came out of his room with his mask, fins, and snorkel. Another

I Don't Want to Keep Sabbath Anymore

missionary, who stood in the hallway with a pair of binoculars around his neck, was flabbergasted. He challenged my friend, "Where do you think you're going?"

"I'm going snorkeling."

"On Sabbath?"

My friend responded kindly, "And where are you going?"

"I'm going bird-watching."

"Tell me," my friend asked, "what day were birds created on?"

"I think it was the fifth day, wasn't it?"

"Yes," my friend replied. And then he set the hook when he asked, "And what day were the fish created on?"

"Also on the fifth day."

The sacred cow was rendered into serious hamburger when my friend said, "You're going bird-watching and I'm going fish-watching."

The second missionary stood silently for a moment and then responded, "Have a great Sabbath!"

What exactly are the limits of the Sabbath that we find in Scripture?

Do you see how easy it is to fall into the trap of limiting what Sabbath can be, but only because we really mean to do well? What exactly are the limits of the Sabbath that we find in Scripture? Three.

1. The commandment itself states that we're not to do common work, and we're to avoid having others do common work for us (Ex. 20:8-11).

2. We're not to be involved in common commerce and financial exchange (Neh. 13:14-21).

3. We're not to engage in those activities that are completely self-centered and not truly based in building up important relationships (Isa. 58:13, 14).

Every other Sabbath restriction of Scripture was either part of the Mosaic code for Israel's specific behavior leading to the days of the Messiah (for instance, not lighting a fire or not gathering manna) or the demands of the Pharisees, which Jesus got into trouble for ignoring (such as picking grain to nibble or doing acts of healing and benevolence).

Those three lasting restrictions are, as Psalm 119 says, exceedingly broad. But by the same token, they provide a wonderful skeleton upon which we may build marvelous Sabbaths.

It's high time that Sabbathkeeping people quit doing "it"—*keeping* it.

I remember a newly baptized member spending time at our house in Michigan one Sabbath afternoon. We lived on the shore of Lake Huron,

52 Sabbath Activities for Teen Groups

and often we'd have members join us to enjoy the view and the cool lake breezes as the thousand-foot cargo ships floated by.

The man's 5-year-old son picked up a stone and threw it into the lake. The father immediately confronted his son and said, "Oh son, we don't do that on Sabbath."

I pulled the father aside and said, "Look, I don't want to undermine your authority with your son or anything, but can you tell me why we don't throw stones into the lake on Sabbath?"

"Well, no. I just figured we shouldn't, and I was embarrassed that the pastor would see my son doing it."

After a few minutes of discussion on what Sabbath should be, all three of us had a pleasant time skipping stones across the lake.

The Sabbath is truly to be a day of creativity. It's to be more than just the memory of God's singular creative acts. It provides us with a forum and the time to enhance and expand our own little remnant of the only drop of divinity we have.

If you only "keep" the Sabbath, you'll never experience that. If you haven't known Sabbath as a joy, it may be because you've lived under all forms of restrictions that have no justification from God's Word. You may be bearing burdens God never intended for you.

Many thinking Jews don't use the term "keeping Sabbath." Their perception is much more accurate when they say that they "make Sabbath." "Making Sabbath" is a creative process. To "make Sabbath" is to move from the mentality of limitation to expansion. "Making Sabbath" puts you in touch with the divine creative entity.

I pray for the day when I have "kept" my last Sabbath. What about you?

I don't want to keep the Sabbath anymore.

Chapter Three

Sabbath Was Never Supposed to Be an Accident!

People who reverence the seventh-day Sabbath call it a "memorial of creation." They proudly state that if the Sabbath had universally been held in its rightful position, there never could have been a theory of evolution. How could you ever mark one day every week for the memory of a God who creates by design and then lose perspective on the Creation event? The Father Himself proclaimed this truth in Exodus 31:12-17.

Because of the Sabbath we remember who is God and who is not. We know that He, by intimate choice, looked down the span of eternity and planned a place for us in it.

Creationists decry the weaknesses in evolution.

We know that the universal law of degeneration (entropy) assumes that all things move from order to chaos and not the reverse.

We point to the fossil and geological record for the absence of supposed missing links to fill in the evolutionary gaps in species differentiation.

We remind the evolutionist of the dilemmas of oxygen presence and absence in the creation and sustaining of DNA.

We point to the Incas, Aztecs, and Egyptians as evidence that society is apparently not destined to progress. Those people who once led the earth in scientific, astronomical, and engineering understanding now have given birth to generations who can't even read or write.

We point out that both evolution and the Genesis Creation accounts

52 Sabbath Activities for Teen Groups

demand faith, but the only faith necessary for Creation is to believe that there's a God who is capable of doing what the Scripture states.

We deplore the assumption that life as we know it and even the entire universe are the result of a fortuitous accident—as evolutionists suggest.

Yes, Sabbath Creationists know better. We can really be smug.

And then we tend to let the Sabbath evolve! You see, if the Sabbath is truly a day to remember Creation and the one weekly reminder that we're only partially divine because of the drop of creativity implanted in us, then the Sabbath should never be allowed to become a weekly accident.

It's sad that many Sabbath "keepers" are truly more evolutionist than creationist in their view of Sabbath, because Sabbath observance becomes something of an accident itself. Accidents are things that happen without planning. I'm quite sure that you'd agree that generally accidents aren't positive events.

Nothing that requires effort, design, planning, and investment can be called an accident. So Sabbath-evolution speaks of a cosmos that's only the result of universal accident or happenstance, whereas Creation demands design. Sabbath-evolution guarantees no specific end or result, but Creation has a predetermined goal for its activity. Sabbath-evolution erases the necessity of the Maker, while Creation cannot exist without Him. Sabbath-evolution comes up to Friday night and says, "I guess we'll see what happens this Sabbath," but Creation takes the time to dream, to plan, and to invest in a specific return for the investment. Sabbath-evolution allows Sabbath to evolve without design, by accident, albeit Creation guarantees advance work as well as a rich return for the time taken to plan it and bring it to fulfillment.

How many accidents in life are good? How many of your Sabbaths are really good? Is there a possible correlation?

The Lord attempted to show this reality in the teaching enactment of the manna story. Unless you put forth the planned effort to prepare for Sabbath, you'd come up to it and find your table empty. The only hope you had for a fulfilling day was by preparing for it.

If any Sabbath ends up hollow and empty, I can be assured that I didn't put forth the investment to plan for the day.

And that gets us back to the purpose of this book. I've had the privilege of dealing with Sabbath issues with thousands of teens and young adults throughout the world. I've known great and rewarding Sabbaths. I've also known some Sabbath experiences that were absolutely rock bottom.

Sabbath as a rich repast or Sabbath as dog food—it's my choice.

I know that many parents, youth leaders, teachers, and pastors wish Sabbath to be more but feel frustrated in not having a resource to assist them in making it rich. So in this book I offer some. Many of them are

Sabbath Was Never Supposed to Be an Accident!

pretty much my own original creation. Some have been adapted from ideas of friends and students. Each has either worked in some format, or I'm itching to try it as an adaptation of something else that I've used. Not every one of them will work in every circumstance. Some are geared to smaller groups, whereas others are designed for mass usage.

That's where your gift of creativity comes into play. Use any of these ideas as a springboard for what will work in your circumstance. I just wanted to provide a skeleton of 52 creative Sabbaths so that the day can truly provide a year of jubilation for those who love the day.

The format is simple. I briefly describe the event, explain the preparation necessary, give the step-by-step how to, and tell how I've seen it accomplished. Some of the ideas will require a small expense, but all will absolutely demand some investment of effort and planning. That's what creation is all about.

I'd be honored to hear from anyone who utilizes some of the ideas, and hear what worked for you, what didn't, and how you adapted things to your own unique situation. It's my prayer that God will use these ideas to honor Himself and His people with many, many rich experiences.

Until we celebrate them together around the glorious mountain of God—happy Sabbath!

**Part 2
Sabbath Activities**

Sabbath Activity One

Adopt a Student Missionary

Theme and Rationale:
Many church leaders are increasingly concerned about "the graying of the church." It's obvious that we'd do well to encourage youth participation and activity in every way we can. For more than 30 years the student missions movement has been one of the most positive outreaches this church has tried.

It appears that most of the students who have served in this capacity have remained active and involved in the church after their tenure was completed. But it's lonely out there in Lower Podunkia.

This activity attacks the problem at two levels: (1) It shows the student missionary that the larger church cares, and (2) it shows the youth who participate that there's a larger church to care about.

Minimum Time Required:
1 to 2 hours

Preparation and Materials:
The first thing needed is the name or names of a student missionary/missionaries and the appropriate address(es). This is a more successful event if the recipients chosen aren't known by the group sending the package. There's a greater benefit for disinterested caring and seeing the larger picture of a world church. It also means more to the one receiving the package to know that strangers cared enough to do this. Names can be acquired from the chaplain's office at any of our colleges.

Generally I've preferred to get the name of someone who is out there

Adopt a Student Missionary

"alone" and not part of a mini-America group at one of the English language compounds.

Urge your participants to plan for this event for a week. Let them gather lightweight, nonperishable items of their choosing. Hard candy, erasers, a Sunday paper, recent *Insight* magazines, stickup notepads. Allow them to be creative. Have them ask, "What would I wish to get if I were out in the middle of nowhere, 10,000 miles from home?"

The leader needs to provide a medium-sized, heavy-duty box, a cassette recorder, and a blank cassette.

How To:

At the specified time have the group sit in a circle around the empty box with the tape recorder in the middle of the table (ready to record). Turn on the machine and then have all in the circle introduce themselves and tell what they're putting in the box. Then just let the activity develop. The group can sing songs, tell the best recent joke they've heard, talk about latest sports developments, describe each other, ask questions of the student missionary . . . whatever.

As the tape is ending have someone close with a prayer of commitment and with a blessing for the student missionary. The tape is then put into the box, and the box is sealed and prepared for shipping.

How It Has Worked:

This has been done with one small group, six groups from one academy, 20 groups at a union leadership conference, etc. It has *always* worked, and the responses from the student missionaries have been expressions of incredible gratitude.

Sabbath Activity Two

Quadrant Art

Theme and Rationale:
Those who have natural abilities in drawing enjoy showing the results of their talent and having them displayed at the front of the room, but those of us who don't have one drop of artistic ability have always hated assignments that only guarantee our public failure. Also "fine art" is generally a singular and individual activity. Quadrant art attacks both issues. It allows even the worst of the artists to have a productive, successful chance at participating in creating something unique and quite beautiful. It's a nonthreatening fine art event that builds concepts of teamwork and mutual support.

Minimum Time Required:
The length of one CD or cassette tape.

Preparation and Materials:
The leader must first find a picture that's very detailed and has a great deal of graphic variety. Some of the old beast pictures of Daniel's prophecies provide great opportunity for something like this. Graphic portrayals from Revelation Seminar brochures work well also.

Draw lines on the picture that will divide it into equal squares (as though you were cutting a sheet cake). You'll want to base the size of the squares on the number of participants you expect. Turn the picture over, and consecutively number each piece so that you'll be able to re-assemble the pieces once they're cut apart. (It would be best to have some of the numbers written sideways, upside down, etc. to make it more difficult for the participants to piece it together before the appropriate time.) The picture is then cut into the squares.

You'll also need to provide plain paper (preferably 10" x 12"), pen-

Quadrant Art

cils, erasers, a pencil sharpener, table space to draw on, and background music.

How To:

Without allowing the group to see the original picture, give each participant a few sheets of blank paper, the pencils, and one piece of the master picture. Tell them that they'll have the time period of the one CD or cassette tape to transpose the piece of art that they have on their small master square onto the larger sheet of paper. Don't allow them to combine pieces and see the larger picture until the activity is completed.

When the music ends, the smaller pieces are joined together again and then the larger pieces are taken in numerical order and taped together as a mural. Obviously some will be darker and some will be lighter; some will be very detailed and others will be more general. The variety portrayed is always interesting.

Depending upon the time budgeted, you may wish to "deprogram" the group on teamwork and the part that each piece plays in the puzzle. This exercise provides an excellent springboard for discussions of unity and uniqueness.

How It Has Worked:

This is a good, nonthreatening event for those who normally are intimidated by art. It's clean; it's simple; it's inexpensive!

I've found that if the group is larger than 16, you'll want to provide more than one picture. (It's obvious that this can be adjusted for the number of participants and doesn't need to be done by exactly 9 or 16 or 25. One person can do two nonadjoining squares, etc.)

Sabbath Activity Three

Bible Sand Sculpture Contest

Theme and Rationale:
 This activity, based upon Bible stories, provides opportunity for creativity and the use of imagination. It's an excellent team challenge, and if you live in a warm climate it's a particularly refreshing Friday night activity under the stars.
 It also is a good exercise to encourage preparation for Sabbath. If the participants are aware of it, they can invest time in planning for it and come well prepared to accomplish something remarkable.

Minimum Time Required:
 The length of one CD or cassette tape.

Preparation and Materials:
 The majority of preparation for this exercise is simply making the participants aware of the event and then finding a location appropriate for it. A reserved sand volleyball court is an excellent venue if you aren't lucky enough to have your own beach. (This could also be transposed to a snow sculpture program, but the issue of keeping everyone warm and dry might be problematic. If someone ended up cold or wet or the target of snowballs, it could put a damper on the effectiveness of what you're intending to accomplish.)
 The participants themselves bring whatever materials they wish in order to enhance their sculpture. You may wish to provide simple sandbox tools or old cups, etc. for those who didn't think to bring them.

Bible Sand Sculpture Contest

How To:

Shortly before the event you'll want to make sure the sand is a little damp so that it can be worked more easily.

Have the group break into teams that please them. Usually four or five per team is the absolute limit. Then tell them that they have the length of one CD or cassette tape to create a sand sculpture based on a biblical theme.

If you want to make it a contest, you can explain that the sculptures will be judged on creativity, artistic endeavor, most easily recognizable as portraying the Bible story, etc. Then let them have a chance at it.

At the end of the tape ask everyone to sit or stand in a circle around the sculptures so that they can be viewed together. At that point you may wish to talk about the sculptures, award prizes, sing songs, etc.

How It Has Worked:

This has been a wonderful large group event. Some of the creativity and artistry demonstrated has been marvelous. Some of the least expected people have created the most magnificent sculptures, and generally participants are astounded at what they see develop from this.

It's become a tradition at one school where I started this. The Sand Sculpture Contest is an annual event, which students anticipate eagerly and enjoy.

On the campus the church members will leave services the next day to wander among the sculptures on Sabbath afternoon, and it generally takes days before anyone begins to break them down.

(One note of warning: If you use a sand volleyball court, you'll want to make sure that all foreign objects are removed at the end of the event. The sand needs to remain clean for the safety of the players.)

Sabbath Activity Four

Cake Art

Theme and Rationale:
Cake art offers a pleasant opportunity to plan, design, and use group interaction in reviewing Scripture stories and then to do something productive with them.

Minimum Time Required:
One half to one hour for creation and then the time required for outreach.

Preparation and Materials:
You'll need to determine the number of participants and then provide an undecorated sheet cake for each group of five or six.

You'll also wish to collect a large variety of items that can be used to decorate the sheet cakes. Typical items might include icing, candies, candles, food coloring, etc. But you can be even more creative (and healthful) by using orange slices, nuts, coconut, raisins, etc. All the items for decoration should be edible.

The groups will need space and materials.

You'll also wish to determine a target group with whom to share the cakes upon the completion of the exercise. This could be a nursing home group, a school for the deaf, etc.

How To:
Put an undecorated cake on a table along with a large variety of items for decorating it. Challenge the group to decorate the cake in a method that tells a Bible story. Each cake should have a team of no more than five people working on it. (You, as the facilitator, need to be aware that some people tend to dominate activities like this. Be particu-

Cake Art

larly sensitive to mixing adults with youth. The adults often feel a need to establish their posture by taking over.) Participants may be allowed to listen to music or a story tape while they are working on their cake.

It will work most effectively if your groups have a sizable space to work in. It's best to have no mingling during the time of the activity. (This avoids many problems, such as the frustration of ideas being copied or someone distracting another group.)

At the end of the allotted time let each group admire the works of the others and then share the cakes with your target groups.

How It Has Worked:

Cake art has proved to be a positive intergenerational event. The creativity sparked by it has been quite astounding, and people of all ages seem to enjoy it.

One of the most unusual instances that I observed was a group that dug a "trench" through the middle of the pan and mounded it up along the edges to create the illusion of the Red Sea crossing.

It's also curious to note how each cake takes on the personality of the group. Some are conservative and very defined, whereas others become exotic and exceedingly symbolic in their art form.

Taking the cakes to a target group allows opportunity for some non-threatening outreach and interaction. It's a good way to show groups in your community that your church knows that religion can be fun.

Sabbath Activity Five

Reminiscent Therapy

Theme and Rationale:
Larry Yeagley proved to me that this is, perhaps, the most positive activity for intergenerational involvement. It provides an opportunity for cooperation and interaction between youth and some mature citizens in a nursing home without droning the standard "What a Friend We Have in Jesus."

Many elderly people can't remember what they had for breakfast, because they have lousy short-term memory. But at the same time, they have very vivid awareness of situations from their youth, because long-term memory has remained acute. Little wonder it's more comfortable for them to live in the past.

Reminiscent therapy starts from the point of reference with which these folks are most comfortable and moves them toward a real vibrancy in the present.

Youth enjoy this activity because they make some fascinating friends and get to see vibrancy return to these senior citizens in a short period of time.

Minimum Time Required:
About one hour.

Preparation and Materials:
You'll need to find a location, preferably a skilled nursing facility, that will allow your group to invade its privacy. The managing director, recreation director, or social activities director would be the person to work through. The facility needs to understand when you intend to come, what you intend to do, and the number of guests that its people are going to be dealing with.

You'll need to collect a series of old items to be put into a brown

Reminiscent Therapy

paper bag. Some ideas: a Brownie camera, a flatiron, some home-canning materials, a pocket watch, or any other simple item that has been long replaced by better technology. (These items don't need to be expensive. They can be basic antique junk.)

How To:

Seat your youth in every other chair of a circle created by the residents. Initially there will be mutual discomfort, but that will dissipate as soon as you begin to pull out the items one by one. All you need to do is hold up the item in the view of the residents and ask them to describe what the item is and what they remember about it.

Allow one or two residents to share a memory about the camera or corset hook or whatever and then give a moment for each of your teens to interact with his or her "partner" about the item. Before they're completely finished, call them back to attention and pull out another item.* Go through the same process for each item in your bag.

When you've completed your inventory, have some leading questions for the youth to ask, such as:

"Who was your favorite president?"

"What was the first car you remember your family having?"

"Did you ever live in a home with a wood stove? Where?"

At the end thank the people for their input and have prayer with them.

How It Has Worked:

Reminiscent therapy seems to work miracles. It's nonthreatening for all involved, and it peels years off of old people and breaks down the barriers for the young. They find that these folks have something to offer and knowledge to share. It's a predetermined win-win situation. And it beats the old Sunshine Band genre to shreds.

---

*In all group activities, particularly those involving youth, you'll find that you gain a psychological advantage by *never* allowing them quite enough time to finish. It does create some frustration, but it also guarantees that they'll never be sitting around feeling like there's nothing to do but be bored. If they don't have enough time, they feel as though they must have really been interested and involved.

Sabbath Activity Six

Play Dough Idols

Theme and Rationale:
This activity is an excellent lead-in to discussions regarding the foolishness of idolatry and issues beyond the simple prohibition of the second commandment. It also sets the tone for dealing with deeper issues of the affection focus and what role God holds in each individual's life.

One of the benefits of this exercise is that shaping and molding colored clay is a very childlike activity and allows great creativity without threatening those who feel somewhat deficient in artistic abilities.

Minimum Time Required:
About one hour.

Preparation and Materials:
You'll need to provide sufficient clay designed for children for your group. (Play-Doh modeling clay is one of the obvious brands of this material.)

There are also recipes for making your own. (See activity 33.) In some ways that would be a better choice, because making the clay could be the first part of the activity and would allow for even more enhanced creativity, as your group would be able to experiment with coloration, etc.

You'll also need to have a space conducive to a childlike activity like this.

How To:
After the clay has been made or provided, each person is assigned to make an idol of his or her own design and creation. The key is to not only create the idol but also share exactly what benefit this idol would

Play Dough Idols

be for those who might worship it. (Baal was supposed to bring rain, and Ra brought the earth back to life from the netherworld of the night.) Tell them they have 20 minutes to accomplish the task.

After the allotted time each person is to share the following:

"My idol's name is . . ."

"It looks like this because . . ."

"My idol's role is to . . ."

After the last idol has been introduced, the discussion is then directed to the foolishness of idolatry. Leading questions for this discussion could include:

Why would anyone worship something that he or she created?

Can people "idolize" the God of heaven? How?

What is the real object of worship in idolatry?

What are deeper implications in the real message of the second commandment?

How It Has Worked:

This has worked with upper elementary students and even adults. Children younger than 10 aren't really capable of dealing with the deeper issues of the assignment. (About the only benefit they can derive from this is to make the idols and then have fun smashing them to show their powerlessness.)

One word of advice—without appropriate deprogramming, you really open the door to criticism from people who tend to be restrictive in the latitude they allow for creativity. The object of the exercise must be absolutely obvious, or you'll set yourself up for some frustrating accusations from those who tend to be sensitive.

FSA-3

Sabbath Activity Seven

The Guilt Backpack

Theme and Rationale:

I'm grateful to a rabbi friend who sparked my mind in this issue. He asked, "If you're going on a journey of 70 years, how much baggage do you want in your backpack?"

An excellent question!

This activity is a three-part challenge relating to the amount of guilt we tend to carry and the foolish ways we try to assuage that guilt.

Minimum Time Required:

Probably two hours.

Preparation and Materials:

You'll need to rent and have cued to the appropriate place in the film or the video *The Mission*. (Yes, it's a standard Hollywood production, and there may be some sensitivity initially to your using it on Sabbath, but not for anyone who takes part in the event!)

You'll need to get a regular backpack and fill it with items that remind you of mistakes in your own life—anything that triggers a memory for you of some failure in the past.

How To:

Part 1

Have the group seated comfortably so that they can see the video after you finish part 1 without a lot of mood-breaking commotion.

Take the backpack and begin to pull out the items one at a time, and relate the mistake or regret of your life that caused you to put it in there. Don't go into great detail or mass confession over grave errors of your life. Just speak of simple regrets and failures. (You'll seriously diminish

The Guilt Backpack

the effectiveness of this if you get too confessional, because your sins and revelations will become the focus rather than the broader issues of guilt and regret. Your group doesn't need to take an inventory of your life.) With some items you may just pull them out of the bag and say, "Oh, I remember that . . . how stupid of me!" or "My dad would know what this one is about . . . ," etc.

The object is not confession, but setting the tone.

Part 2

Immediately start the 10- or 12-minute section of *The Mission* in which Rodrigo is chased by his brother, they have the confrontation, and Rodrigo kills him—*not* the 30 seconds before, in which his brother is in bed with the lady. (It's about a fourth of the way into the film.) Continue the video until the national cuts the baggage loose from Rodrigo and the scene ends with him crying in relief. Turn off the video and . . .

Part 3

Immediately ask the group to share their earliest childhood memory of guilt. ("When was the first time in your life that you felt guilt?")

After each one has shared (and some of them will really be cute), ask the clincher question: "What things do people do to assuage guilt or to rid themselves of the burden of guilt?"

The self-directed end of this discussion will be finding that the Scripture answer of giving guilt away is the only healthy option for someone who doesn't want to spend 70 years with a massive load.

How It Has Worked:

This group involvement activity has had a powerful effect every time I have used it. The backpack analogy is so very simple and the portrayal of *The Mission* is so graphic and provocative that even the most hardened sit-in-the-back-and-giggle types are drawn into the issue. This is simply a wonderful trigger event for serious discussion of real scriptural issues.

Warning: I wouldn't advise using the whole film at this (or probably any other) time. The music is haunting, the cinematography is stunning, the story is overwhelming . . . but there's nongratuitous native nudity and graphic violence at the end. The violence is the honest and tragic end to the story, but because of the nudity and the violence you'd probably set yourself up for serious criticism from some conservative elements. Remember: "Be . . . wise as serpents, and harmless as doves" (Matt. 10:16).

Sabbath Activity Eight

The Jerusalem Observer

Theme and Rationale:
The gift shop of the Jerusalem Museum of Art sells a coffee table book that's really fascinating. It's the imaginary front page of various newspapers throughout biblical history—the *Babylonian Times*, the *Nile Review*, the *Syrian Chronicle*, etc.

Each page is a modern representation of Bible stories as though they were contemporary headlines: "Crazy Noah Still at It," "Jericho Falls," "Paul's Ship Lost at Sea," "Three Criminals Executed Outside Jerusalem."

The present activity takes its clue from that book and gives people an opportunity to saturate themselves in Bible stories and bring those stories to life.

Minimum Time Required:
Probably two hours.

Preparation and Materials:
Provide blank paper, at least 11" x 17", pencils, rulers, compasses, etc. Have a few samples of what regular newspaper front pages are like, then provide background music, and get out of the way and watch as the creative juices start to flow.

How To:
Break your group up into teams of not more than three or four people each. Explain to them the concept of creating a front page for a newspaper for the Bible event that they select. Tell them that the finished product should be clean, neat, and chronologically correct. (They can't have God dropping the sixth plague on Pharaoh on the same page as Jonah preaching in Nineveh.) It will work to their

advantage if they pick a single event and build around it.

Remind them that they can include all types of creative things:
Masthead
Headline
Weather corner
Index to other pages
Interview article
Reader response or survey
Auxiliary articles (for example, "Boy Hit by Chariot Dies")
Sports notes ("Jorabalek Goes to Olympics in Athens")
Charts or graphs
Pictures with appropriate captions
Editorial comment on that major Bible story
Price of paper (for instance, "Two Silver Coins")
Date of paper ("Sixth Year of King Bakkanik")

Put on the music and tell them to enjoy! Generally team members will immediately assign themselves tasks (for example, one for artwork, one to write a lead article, one to create the side piece, etc.). You may wish to assist with triggering ideas if a group seems stalled.

Generally this activity works most effectively when it's mostly nondirected.

When the work is completed, these pieces of art can be displayed for your church family or compiled in a notebook for future reference or taken to be shared with shut-ins. You dream up the usage.

How It Has Worked:

Many youth really enjoy being given the freedom to create. Often all they need is encouragement, a few boundaries, and a good challenge.

It's been fun to use this as quasi-competition in which teams of youth and teams of adults contend. You'll find that usually the youth are more effective in this type of work, because the adults are often too busy marking their territory with each other. It's not a bad lesson in cooperation when the adults observe the ease with which the youth negotiate their roles and get into the task with less conflict.

I've often wondered if this could be a mixer event for youth and shut-ins.

Sabbath Activity Nine

The Great Family Switch

Theme and Rationale:
Many times we're so emotionally involved with those who are closest to us that we lose perspective on many things. Parents tend to be more accepting and less demanding of other people's children, and young people often feel that so-and-so's mom or dad really understands me.

The Great Family Switch forces all types of possibilities about those issues in a structured manner. It confronts how we feel about family.

Minimum Time Required:
This is an all-day event.

Preparation and Materials:
Recruit families who are willing to participate in the experiment and then prayerfully match the "Smith kids" with the "Evans parents" and the "Evans kids" with the "Smith parents." (I believe it would predispose a more effective deprogramming if you simply flip-flop families, rather than have the kids of family number 1 with parents number 2 and the parents of family number 1 with the kids of family number 7, etc.)

You also need to prepare for the Saturday night vespers banquet and a "Family Blessing" sheet.

The "Family Blessing" sheet should be a simple response page that allows the parents to reply anonymously to "I really appreciate my kids because . . ." and the kids to respond anonymously to "I really appreciate this about my parents . . ."

How To:
Have all participating families commit to getting together at a prede-

The Great Family Switch

termined location 15 minutes before the church service begins in order to receive their "new family" assignments.

Then they're to sit together for the worship, have lunch together as a family, and spend the afternoon together.

One half hour before sunset they're all to get together for a worship and the banquet. (You might just wish for this banquet to allow everyone to make his or her own haystacks, or pizza muffins, or something that limits the amount of preparation and work.) "Adopted" families are to remain together during the banquet—preferably not at a table where their real family is sitting.

At the end of the meal have the adults move to one side of the room and the youth to the other. Ask one leading question: "Did you find yourself trying harder to impress these kids or parents and make this a good experience for them?" (If people are honest, they'll probably admit that they did.)

Of course, the next obvious question is "Why?" That raises all types of issues.

When you feel you've accomplished enough with those questions, give them five minutes of silence to respond on the sheet that you prepared for each group.

After five minutes gather the anonymous sheets and read them out loud. (As facilitator use your judgment to edit or shape responses to make them as positive as possible.)

When you finish with as many sheets as you choose to read, ask everyone to gather at the center of the room for a prayer for all the families.

It might be nice then to plan the rest of the evening for positive, non-threatening group interaction games, such as Actionary or charades, in which everyone has the opportunity to mingle comfortably.

Be sure that you make the opportunity to thank everyone who was willing to take the risk and be involved.

How It Has Worked:

This is one I haven't tried yet. It's a recent idea, and I'm looking forward to giving this one a shot.

In theory it seems really promising, because we often find that both adults and kids tend to be on their best behavior when they're thrown into a situation like this. The adults want to prove that they're good, funny, creative, and caring parents, and they probably will invest more of their energies in making it a good Sabbath. It should challenge complacency.

Sabbath Activity Ten

Musical Balloons

Theme and Rationale:
We often desire to get people to participate in sharing their feelings and values but are at a loss as to how to get it started or how to trigger people to be involved comfortably.

Musical Balloons offers a way to have a broad spectrum of people take part in this type of sharing in a manner that only seems fast-paced. The reality is that depth can be attained without people feeling that they're being threatened.

Minimum Time Required:
More than an hour would probably *not* be effective.

Preparation and Materials:
Get a number of balloons, and have only one that is an odd color from the rest. (You might use all green balloons except for a red one.)

On small pieces of paper write a number of leading statements:

"When I was a kid, I wanted to be a . . ."
"I want Jesus to return when . . ."
"To me, $___ is the least that I would call a lot of money."
"If I could go back in life to start over, it would be when . . ."
"I'd like to ask God three questions . . ."
"The Bible character I like least is . . ."
"I really like _____ about the person on my right."
"I don't understand why Jesus . . ."
"The first lie I ever told was . . ."
"I'm most afraid of . . ."
"My pet peeve is . . ."
"I get really frustrated with . . ."

Musical Balloons

Those type of statements would be written on individual pieces of paper and put into a balloon. (Sources for questions/statements could be *The Ungame, The Question Book,* or *Is Your Dog Jewish?*)

Also you'll need to provide a cassette or CD player to provide the music, which you'll start and stop for the event.

How To:

Seat all the participants in a circle. Explain that this is like musical chairs except no one is going to get squashed and no chairs are going to be broken. Instead, you'll begin the music and they'll pass the balloons to the right.

When the music stops, the person with the odd-color balloon must take one of the other balloons and pop it. He or she is to read the statement on the piece of paper and then respond to the group.

If you have seven in your group, it's best to have about 15 balloons and replenish them as they get popped. When you get down to an equal number of balloons to people, then you'll begin to eliminate the person who has to pop the balloon—have him or her respond and then move out of the circle.

When the last person remains, he or she pops the odd-color balloon and reads a piece of paper that asks him or her to lead the group in a blessing prayer.

How It Has Worked:

This has been a good event, because it's active without getting anyone hurt or requiring great athletic skills. Almost all of us can hand off a balloon without making fools of ourselves!

It also gets people to open up and reveal themselves in a manner that doesn't appear heavy. It gives a chance for people to reveal their feelings.

There's relatively no age limitation, and this activity works with a broad spectrum of people.

Bonus Idea (no extra charge): If you number the balloons and have them broken in a specific order, they can provide leading questions or verses for a Sabbath school lesson discussion with juniors or earliteens.

Sabbath Activity Eleven

Exposing the Great Lie

Theme and Rationale:

Before softball leagues, fitness clubs, growth seminars, television, and the Arab oil embargo raised gasoline prices from 26.9 cents to more than $1 a gallon, church families used to get together at every possible excuse. The annual six-week evangelistic series seemed to be a social interaction opportunity as much as evangelism. In general, we had the time, and the church was a place for community gathering.

Times have changed in North America, but throughout Latin America this is still true. Church families will spend all day Sabbath together with a string of meetings running one after another.

Often one of those meetings is a doctrinal study and reaffirmation. Exposing the Great Lie is an opportunity to combine the two doctrines that we've been told will be the "testing" issues during the end-time—the Sabbath and the state of the dead.

In exposing Joseph McCarthy's tactics, Harry Truman opened up the concept of "the great lie"—an untruth that's told long enough and loud enough so that it eventually becomes the truth. This Sabbath activity looks at how often we've been saturated with the first lie: "Ye shall not surely die" (Gen. 3:4).

Minimum Time Required:

Probably two hours.

Preparation and Materials:

Obtain and have ready to show specific segments of four movies: *Gandhi*, *A Man Called Horse*, *Rocket Gibraltar*, and *Masada*. Take the time to have them set to the exact place where you wish to begin them. You'll also need a blackboard or overhead projector or some

Exposing the Great Lie

way to display brainstorming responses.

How To:

First, have the group read the following verses—John 11:11-14; Ecclesiastes 9:5, 6, 10; Psalm 136:3, 4; Psalm 6:5; 1 Timothy 6:16; and Hebrews 9:27. Second, establish a consensus that the group believes that after this life a person is unconscious in death until the resurrection. Third, read Genesis 3:1-4 to establish the origin of the great lie.

Then view the following movie segments without comment:

the end of *Gandhi*, from the assassination through the funeral procession.

the end of *A Man Called Horse*, where the death and burial rituals are portrayed.

in *Masada*, from the time the wind shifts until the end of the film (approximately 12 minutes).

in *Rocket Gibraltar*, the ending in which the children discover that Grandpa is dead and sneak the body out until the conclusion in the sunset. (Warning: You may decide that some of the language of *Rocket Gibraltar* is too offensive for your group. It's a powerful addition to this event, but it also comes with a frustrating price exacted by Hollywood.)

At the end of the viewings debrief on how various people view death. Then ask your group to begin listing the titles of movies that have been popular during the past 15 years which teach that you don't really die. The initial titles given will be the obvious: *Ghost* and *Friday the 13th, part 72*, but once they begin to think they'll realize that those represent black magic and that Hollywood has saturated us with the great lie through the attractive representation of white magic in such films as *Field of Dreams*, all the Star Wars/Star Trek genre, *Flatliners*, *All Dogs Go to Heaven*, *Peggy Sue Got Married*, and the list goes on and on. Any film that depicts existence beyond this one is teaching the great lie. Your group will find that they have been inundated with the great lie, and when it comes in the packages called *Field of Dreams*, *The Search for Spock*, or when depicted as an old crusader in the final Indiana Jones movie, it's really attractive. (Don't be naive—90 percent of your group will know all these films well.) You'd do well to end by going back to the original verses again.

How It Has Worked:

When they see for themselves how saturated they've been with the lie, this becomes a most provocative exercise. It has never failed.

Sabbath Activity Twelve

Sukkah Hopping

Theme and Rationale:

This is a nice outdoor activity for the fall of the year (September or October). It opens up a better understanding of Sukkoth (the biblical Feast of Tabernacles) and also exposes your group to interaction with whatever Jewish community exists in your area. It also gives a great opportunity to understand the life and world of Jesus better.

(A sukkah is a temporary booth or shelter built for the Feast of Tabernacles. *Sukkoth* is the Hebrew plural for *sukkah*.)

Minimum Time Required:

Most of Sabbath afternoon.

Preparation and Materials:

You must invest time in researching the location of any observant Jewish families, synagogues, or study centers in your local area. Then you must go in advance to meet with those folks and share what you wish to do, so that you might get their blessing and not surprise them by showing up unannounced. (You'll find that the vast majority of Jews are more than happy to have you participate and will be pleased that you wish this type of nonthreatening interaction.)

You'd also do well to study a bit for yourself on the background of Sukkoth in the Jewish calendar year. The best simple reference work on this, in my opinion, is *The Jewish Catalogue,* by Siegel, Strassfeld, and Strassfeld. (It's an amazing reference for Gentiles.) You must also plan to provide sufficient transportation.

How To:

At a predetermined time (possibly after a potluck or fellowship meal)

Sukkah Hopping

gather your group together for a bit of background on Sukkoth. Share with them what you've learned about a sukkah (booth) and what the Feast of Tabernacles was all about.

Remind them that some of the major events of Jesus' ministry took place at a specific Feast of Tabernacles (John 7-10) and that Christ Himself would have lived in a sukkah outside Jerusalem during the occasion. Point out that this is sort of a "Jewish Christmas tree," because it gives the Jewish children an opportunity to decorate and be creative with the sukkah in much the same way that Christian children do with Christmas trees.

Then just as Christians go on "light tours" during the Christmas season to see decorations, share that they'll be taking part in a very Jewish experience—"sukkah hopping." Many Jews enjoy going around to observe the variety of decorations in the various locations of synagogues and homes.

You'll then go to the prearranged locations to spend time in the various sukkoth and experience the flavor of the celebration. If you've done your homework well, you should have been able to make prearrangements with a rabbi, or some other observant Jew, to show you the elements of the festival (the *Etrog*, the *Lulav*/the four species) and have him share with your group the meaning of the feast and how Jews feel about it.

How It Has Worked:

Because of my degree in Jewish studies I probably have an easier time pulling this off than the average Gentile would, but it has always worked well for me.

I've had Sabbath school classes and elementary children who wanted to go back and create their own Sukkoth celebration afterward.

It's fun, it's clean, and it's enlightening for Christians.

A little advice. It's particularly important to be sensitive to two issues: (1) for some Christians you need to be sure that you've set the biblical basis for this and show Jesus as part of this, or they get really sensitive about "going Jewish," and (2) don't allow anyone to turn this into a "let's go evangelize the Jews today" event! Statements to someone who has graciously invited you to their sukkah, such as "C'mon, in your heart you really know Jesus is the Messiah, don't you?" are rude and demeaning. Make clear to your group what the activity is for and what it is *not* for.

13

Sabbath Activity Thirteen

Dual Jeopardy

Theme and Rationale:
Bible trivia isn't going to save anybody. It will provide little consolation in a time of trouble to know that Samson was buried between Zorah and Eshtaol. But sometimes it's good to have fun with the Bible. And perhaps that in itself serves a purpose.

Minimum Time Required:
Possibly up to two hours.

Preparation and Materials:
Have enough "stick up" note sheets to fill out the rounds of two Jeopardy games. (That's 60 per game. $100, $200, $300, $400, and $500 in six categories for the first round and double those amounts for the six categories of the second round.) Provide 24 "category headings" cards for two games—12 for each game.

It works best if you choose 24 categories to build off of: Moses, the Gospels, Heaven, Bible Animals, Old Testament Women, New Testament Potpourri, Parables, Prophets, David, Paul, Luke 2, the Sanctuary, Gold in the Bible, the Crucifixion, the Flood, the Apostles, Bible Trees, the Tribes of Israel, Plagues, Kings, Priests, Fins and Feathers, Miracles, and Judges would be a good listing to suggest.

How To:
Divide your people into two groups, and separate the groups so that they can't easily be aware of what the other group is doing. Give them time to work in those two large groups to create a Jeopardy game for the other group.

They can resolve who will create the questions (or answers if you re-

Dual Jeopardy

ally want to be technical) from the 12 categories that their group has been assigned. Remind them that the questions/answers should progress from more simple issues to more difficult as they increase in value on the scale. They won't have enough time to discuss all 60 questions/answers together, so they should probably find some way to break up the categories among themselves. You may need to assist in this process.

Remember that people generally feel they've enjoyed a situation more if there wasn't quite enough time or if they felt pressured for time. If they sense that there has been a lag in the event, it psychologically tells them this isn't something really fun.

Then call the two groups together and divide one group into two or three teams. They will then play the Jeopardy game created by the other group.

When the first game is finished, reverse the process and have teams from the second group play the game created for them.

How It Has Worked:

For some reason Jeopardy works. It seems to be fast-paced enough and doesn't put people on the spot (unless they do it to themselves). It gives room for those who aren't really the Bible scholar types to take part and enjoy it also.

As with anything like this, the only area of concern is that the know-it-all might dominate the event. By running it as two separate games and by breaking it into smaller segments for the creation of the games, you defuse that to a degree.

Sabbath Activity Fourteen

The Forum

Theme and Rationale:
Most people don't often get enough opportunity to interact with church leadership in a fulfilling manner. It's really positive to mix with these folks, find out that they're human, and discover that though they don't always agree with each other they do love their church and support each other despite their differences.

Minimum Time Required:
A very defined starting and ending time—probably not more than an hour and a half.

Preparation and Materials:
This event takes leg work or phone work. You must pick a panel of recognized church leaders (that is, conference officers, respected laypeople, pastors, committed business leaders) and then try to lock in a date on which you can get about six of them to commit a Sabbath afternoon to your event. It's obviously best if they're bright, articulate, and think well on their feet.

It's best if you acknowledge a spectrum of people in the church based on position, racial and ethnic concerns, gender concerns, and those who are dependent on the church financially versus those who are not church professionals.

Prepare your group several weeks in advance for the event so that they can be thinking of issues and questions that concern them.

You must also decide if you have the skills necessary to moderate this or if you should ask another to be responsible to make it happen in a positive way.

The Forum

How To:

Have seats on a stage for the five or six panel members and a side position on the stage for the moderator. Have sheets available for those who wish to write questions for the panel. Also appoint one or two ushers, who move around the room to receive the questions and deliver them to the moderator.

The moderator establishes the ground rules from the beginning:

1. This is not a gripe session.
2. This is an opportunity for honesty, but there's no room for any personal attacks or ax grinding.
3. *No questions will be taken directly from the floor. They must be written, and the moderator has the authority to edit a question or statement if necessary for the spirit of the event.* (This is imperative!)
4. There's no guarantee that every issue will be dealt with.
5. Unless it seems appropriate to the moderator, no question or issue will be dealt with by more than three of the panel members.
6. The moderator has the prerogative to move the discussion on to another issue when he or she feels that enough has been said.
7. This event is for the upbuilding of the community of the church, and everything done in it should be for that purpose.

The moderator may start with a few leading seed questions that you've created or have solicited prior to the forum. They should focus on issues of current church discussion (for instance, church finance, social concerns, youth issues, church policies) and have a broad appeal to the concerns of those in attendance.

Unless there's a very specific reason to continue beyond the set time allowed, it's imperative that the forum be closed at the time predetermined.

How It Has Worked:

The moderator is the key to this. If he or she keeps it lively and positive, allowing the panel members to show their hearts and the variety of their feelings, it's a great exercise.

I've seen it work marvelously at camp meetings, on academy campuses, at youth retreats, collegiate gatherings, and Sabbath schools.

It's not a bad lesson at all to see the panel disagree in love.

FSA-4

15

Sabbath Activity Fifteen

Young Mother's Lifelines

Theme and Rationale:
The church family consists of subgroups who have special needs. Often the church at large isn't really sensitive to the specific issues confronting some of these subgroups.

One group to focus on for Sabbath involvement could be the mothers who have very small children. Everyone wants to cuddle babies or small children as long as they're attractive, quiet, smiling, and don't have a diaper that's far past changing.

A young mother doesn't often need compliments—she needs help. This is particularly true if she is, for whatever reason, holding the fort by herself during a worship service.

If we truly wish to be a church that consistently encourages young children to be in our worship services, it seems we should do all we can to make those services attractive and user-friendly to children and the mothers who struggle with them.

Minimum Time Required:
Maybe up to two hours.

Preparation and Materials:
It will take a commitment of time to collect a variety of materials that can be set out for this project. You'll be looking for things that are quiet, colorful, child-safe, durable, and cheap.

Obvious suggestions would be cloth, papers, magazines, straws, large buttons, pipe cleaners—all manner of craft items that meet the criteria. You'll also wish to provide means for connecting some of the materials together: yarns, glues, etc.

I think it's always nice to have some background sound for events

Young Mother's Lifelines

like this. A good CD, cassette, or perhaps an interesting story tape usually fills the bill. (You might be surprised how universally people relate to listening to a story, especially if it's really creative and well done. James Dobson's Focus on the Family has resources like this, as does your local public library.)

How To:

All you need is the material, the space, and an environment that encourages creativity.

Explain the problem to your group, and tell them to resolve it with the materials provided. Often creativity sparks creativity, and you'll find that once the juices start flowing, people will really get into something like this.

Remind the group that the products they create must be quiet and safe for small children.

How It Has Worked:

Usually exercises like this always amaze me. I often don't hold out a lot of hope but am consistently surprised (and rewarded) by the amount of creativity demonstrated in the solutions produced. I usually say to myself, "Why didn't I think of something like that?"

Another common result of this type of event is that you don't just "fill" a Sabbath afternoon, but you create a greater awareness within those who participate. You may very well find some of the participants volunteering to assist after they give away their "quiet toys."

It's a good thing to aim at one target and surprise yourself by hitting about six!

16

Sabbath Activity Sixteen

The Observant Communion

Theme and Rationale:
It's said that tradition is the "dead religion of living people" and that ritual is the "living religion of dead people."

Communion can be just another tradition or a wonderful and really vibrant ritual.

This activity involves a beautiful enactment of the precious ritual of Communion.

Minimum Time Required:
Probably an hour or more.

Preparation and Materials:
In our denomination only ordained elders are authorized to lead out in the sacred Communion service. If you aren't an ordained elder, you'll wish to defuse any possible criticism by asking one to assist you in this event.

You'll need to provide enough grape juice for all your participants to have a glassful if they choose and enough basins and towels for all to participate in the foot washing if they desire.

For the bread I'd advise making loaves that can be torn. I use the simple Jewish method for matzo used at the Seder (the home Passover service). They're large, flat loaves that look like pizza dough or pita.

The recipe is simple: three parts whole-wheat flour, one part water, a sprinkling of salt, and a few drops of olive oil. From the time that you begin mixing the ingredients until the bread is out of the oven cannot be more than 18 minutes, little wonder they call it "quick bread!"

Mix the ingredients and put them on a large, flat pan; bake in an oven at 500° F.

The Observant Communion

How To:

After some appropriate singing, have the leader share that this will be an unusual Communion service. Ask one person (preferably the pastor, a teacher, or another acknowledged servant/leader) to select five people from the group whom he or she will ask to serve in foot washing. (Don't be foolish by setting yourself up for criticisms—same sex choices!)

The servant takes all his or her "disciples" to the front and seats them in a row of chairs. The group sings or other music is provided while they observe the foot washing. Don't be in a hurry with this. Let the servant take his or her time and have a personal event with each of the individuals.

After all five have been served, quiz the participants. Ask the "servant" what it was like to give without receiving. Let him or her speak of how it felt physically. (You'll often find that the knees and the back hurt, teaching something about Jesus' washing of the feet of the twelve).

Ask the "disciples" how they felt about receiving without giving. Ask them what it felt like to be "observed."

Then ask the "audience" how they felt about the event.

When the depths of the experience have been plumbed, open up the opportunity for any to participate in the foot washing. Some may also choose to participate with more than one. Let them know in advance that they have a set time of about 20 minutes to do this.

At the end of the foot washing, go immediately to the Lord's Supper emblems. The only change in this is that the participants should be allowed to "break" the symbol of the body themselves and receive a full cup of the blood symbol so that they may savor it slowly.

Upon the conclusion of the Lord's Supper, sing an appropriate hymn.

How It Has Worked:

I've used this form of Communion about once a year with church families, academy groups, at church retreats, to conclude Weeks of Prayer, at union youth rallies, singles weekends, etc. It *always* evokes deep responses and rich, meaningful participation.

Many people have left this event saying, "Communion has never meant so much to me, and I don't want to forget this." Even those who normally don't participate jealously seem to want to remember it.

I've seen this Communion bring the upper room to life. Who can ask for more?

Sabbath Activity Seventeen

Making a Mezuzah

Theme and Rationale:

In Deuteronomy 6:4-9 the Lord admonished that His people should find ways to make the covenant agreement a constant reality. One of the ways this has been fulfilled is by marking the doorposts of the observant with a mezuzah.

If you want to see the best of Jewish creativity, visit a Jewish bookstore or a synagogue gift shop. (Unless you'd like to take me to Jerusalem so that I can give you a tour of the shops in Mea Shearim!) Artistic endeavor in Judaism is best displayed in ritual objects because of the dilemmas of the prohibition of the second commandment.

There are three stipulations for making a mezuzah kosher (fit/acceptable):

1. It must enclose a little scroll bearing a specified portion of the Scriptures. This miniature scroll is called a *klaff*.

2. It must have the Hebrew letter *shin* displayed on the outside. The *shin* looks something like an English "W" and is the first letter in one of the titles of God, El Shaddai (made famous among Christians by Michael Card and Amy Grant).

3. It must be made of a permanent material and nailed to the right-side doorpost at an angle.

The mezuzah is a sign to those who live in the home and to those who pass by the home that this is a place marked for observance to God.

This Sabbath exercise allows the participants to feel somewhat like Bezaleel and Aholiab.

Minimum Time Required:

Probably an hour or more.

Making a Mezuzah

Preparation and Materials:

You'll need to provide a variety of permanent materials (glass, clay, wood, plastics, etc.) for the body of the mezuzah and then a variety of items to decorate and mark it. It can be marked by other permanent materials mounted on the exterior, etched, carved, painted, etc.

You'll also want to provide a small piece of paper for the individualized creation of the *klaff*.

How To:

It's best to first spend a few moments with the text of Deuteronomy to show what inspired the idea of the mezuzah. Then you may wish to show samples of it that you have been able to obtain or borrow or take pictures of.

When the group has a feeling for what the mezuzah is all about, turn them loose to create their own individualized mezuzah. If someone is a tennis nut, he or she may wish to shape it like a racquet. Someone else may wish to make it look ancient, while some may wish to be very simple and contemporary in their design. The only rules are the three defined criteria.

It probably would be most meaningful for each participant to pick out his or her own scriptural passage for the *klaff*. The intention isn't to create something quasi-Jewish, but to provide the opportunity for the participants to make something very personalized and meaningful.

If there's some particular sensitivity about the Jewish nature of this, they may wish to steal the idea and create something decidedly Christian.

As with many exercises like this, background music always enriches the atmosphere. It creates another sensory blessing.

How It Has Worked:

Because the rules for this are so loose, this is a great exercise for creativity. When the participants finish, they've not only learned something but also have their own piece of art to remind them of what they've thought and whom they want to be.

Students frequently mount these mezuzahs on their dorm room doors, and church members display them in their homes.

Sabbath Activity Eighteen

Window Murals

Theme and Rationale:

Certain things evoke responses in us: the aroma of homemade bread or soup; the sound of the individual trumpeter playing taps; a soft, warm blanket fresh from the dryer; a specific old hymn; or the smell of burning leaves. To victims, certain triggers bring memories and sensations of pain and fear, but many sensory triggers can bring positive, warm memories.

The sight of vibrant stained glass evokes a sense of reverence and sacredness. Pale, washed-out apologies of pastels and plastic don't accomplish this. In order to really get this done the colors need to be rich and deep, leaning heavily on reds, blues, purples, deep greens, and golds.

I personally enjoy making stained glass, but that's an art and craft that many will never have the joy of creating themselves. A window mural is an inexpensive creation that allows a large group of people to participate in something like a stained-glass creation. Taking the project from dream to completion is a particularly fulfilling exercise.

Minimum Time Required:

Not less than two hours.

Preparation and Materials:

You'll need to provide a wide variety of inexpensive latex paints in deep, rich colors. Also have sufficient brushes, newspaper or drop cloths, and pencils to write on glass.

If you have reservations concerning your group's ability to visualize stained glass, you may wish to pick up a few sample books at a stained-glass or craft shop. Many coloring books found in Christian bookstores will show something like this, or seasonal coloring books in variety stores will provide ideas.

Window Murals

It's obvious that you'll need to make arrangements with your church or school or someone who has a number of large windows or glass doors so that you'll have a place to do the murals.

How To:

Forewarn your group to come prepared to paint. (There's no need to risk a new Sabbath dress for this!)

A few exhibits of stained glass should be enough inspiration for them to be ready to tackle the project. Make them aware that the one thing that will cause this to look more like the stained-glass genre in contrast to the old painted window at the local supermarket is the planned presence of the black lines between the colors called "lead came."

The project will be more viable if you've picked a prearranged theme or motif for the panels. They should be done as a series. The number of doors or windows could determine your theme. (Seven doors would lend themselves to the days of Creation, 12 could be tribes of Israel, five could be five of Jesus' miracles, three could represent the Trinity, etc.)

After the group divides into teams and the appropriate assignments have been made, it's best if the leader or facilitator is consistently available to make suggestions, resolve problems, or just keep the exercise upbeat and moving. Try not to do their work for them. How can they be creative if you do the work? Good leadership inspires and allows.

Obviously some of the work will be stunning, and some will be a bit less remarkable. The inspiration and teamwork are more valuable here than the perfection of the finished product. In a project like this a good spirit and positive Sabbath feelings are of much greater value than whether *you* are completely satisfied with the end result.

How It Has Worked:

This is a recent idea for me, and I've yet to have the opportunity to give it a shot. I think it has real promise, and look forward to implementing it someday.

Sabbath Activity Nineteen

The Great "Love" Mixer

Theme and Rationale:
Isn't it curious that whenever we hear people refer to "the Elijah message," it seems to sound as though their perception of this theme is one of very specific demands, a division of the camp, and some angry prophet somewhere "calling sin by its right name"? Perhaps we need to read Malachi again. The Elijah theme of Malachi isn't just one of purging and purifying, but also one of unity. Elijah isn't specifically referred to until the last two verses of chapter 4.

Don't you find it infinitely more appealing to realize that this end-time message will be one that turns the hearts of the fathers to the children and the hearts of the children to the fathers? Wouldn't you give your right arm for that?

It would seem that we might predispose the day of Elijah (and the concurrent day of the Lord) by getting this message back in balance. While multitudes may wish to press for purging, I'd rather find what it takes to get a son's heart back to beating in harmony with his father's!

The Great "Love" Mixer helps in that process. It reminds the older generation that they were once youth, and it teaches the youth that the older ones were once young and immature!

Minimum Time Required:
Depending on the size of the group, at least an hour.

Preparation and Materials:
Only a comfortable space in which adults can sit facing their youth.

How To:
This is an incredibly easy and self-generating activity. Don't let the

The Great "Love" Mixer

simplicity of it fool you. This is a powerful exercise.

All that's needed is a good mix of teens to young adults and a cluster of their parents and other married elders. You seat them comfortably so that each group faces the other, and then you ask two leading questions:

1. Would you each tell us the circumstances of
    how you met your spouse?
    about your dating?
    the length of your courtship?
    and how you proposed to her, or how he proposed to you?

Then allow each person/couple to answer in their own style and timing. Generally the stories will be fascinating. Some will be astoundingly surprising, and many will be a riot. Very few couples experience the expected "traditional" dating to marriage scene. That expectation usually proves to be a myth.

This first segment is often a real eye-opener. Many youth will look at their parents and elders and laughingly say, "If I ever did that you'd kill me!"

After the first question has been satisfactorily explored, move on to the second question:

2. Would you please tell us about your honeymoon?

The stories will often bring the whole group to tears with laughter. Many have experienced breakdowns, lousy weather, everything that could go wrong and more. (And the younger generation will find that a two-week trip to the Bahamas isn't necessarily the guaranteed prerequisite for a marriage that makes it.)

This event will end when the discussions wind down. It's probably psychologically stronger if there's no heavy moral of the story or commitment issue. It's probably most effective to allow this exercise to remain light, letting each person glean from it the benefit for himself or herself. End it by simply thanking everyone for being there and sharing in the fun.

How It Has Worked:

I've never seen it fail. Both sides gain a new insight into the other.

The young view the older generation in a new perspective, and it reminds the older ones of when they were "young and dumb." With those insights a new appreciation and acceptance can grow. Elijah is assisted in doing his work!

Sabbath Activity Twenty

Scripture Acrostics Game

Theme and Rationale:
Sabbath games can be a positive event of social interaction, learning, and enjoyment, or they can deteriorate to be fillers for the time when you can't do anything else.

If they're only time fillers or something to occupy those who haven't gotten into the habit of sleeping the Sabbath hours away, then you have to wonder if they do any good at all. It isn't often that group games and creativity get blended.

The Scripture Acrostics Game can help create one of those rare occasions.

Minimum Time Required:
Probably an hour.

Preparation and Materials:
Only blank paper with pens or pencils, and the space for four teams to work individually for a while and then join in one central location.

How To:
Break your group into four teams that represent an appropriate mix of age, maturity, skill, knowledge of the Bible, etc. When they get back together, they'll try to get their partner team (1 and 3, 2 and 4) to guess the acrostic before the opponent teams do. After showing them examples, give each group the assignment to create 10 Scripture acrostics.

Here are some samples:

No land in sight
Only water, water everywhere

Ruling the world
Oppressing all enemies

Scripture Acrostics Game

All the animals are restless.

Hold on, here comes another wave!

Look, my grandsons dress funny!
Each one wears white.
Very busy, morning and evening
I'm the father of the priesthood.

Making life tough, even for friends
Everyone fears me!

Perhaps I'll try.
Everyone else is afraid.
There's another wave coming.
Easy does it.
Right now I wish I'd worked more on my backstroke!

Ladies don't usually run businesses here.
You know my favorite color.
Do you have church on the beach?
I help lead our prayer group.
All of Philippi knows me.

Those are simple examples, but these rules make it more definitive:

1. Each clue from the appropriate letter must make sense from the story of the thing named in the acrostic. (No generic "I'm a nice guy.")

2. A round will consist of each team reading one word. The words will be read one clue at a time. After the clue is read, 10 seconds will be given for a guess, and any team may respond one time during those 10 seconds. If the acrostic is guessed after the first letter clue, the guessing team gets 50 points, 45 for the second letter, 40 for the third, etc. If a "partner team" guesses correctly (that is, team 3 gets the full word of team 1), a bonus of 20 points is given.

3. To keep people from just shouting out any word that starts with that letter, wrong guesses count a minus 20 points.

4. At the end of each round, the moderator will award a bonus 30 points to the team that had the most creative acrostic of that round.

How It Has Worked:

This is a new creation for me, and I look forward to trying it soon. I'd assume that the age span for really having success at this would be from 12 on up. Feel free to adapt the rules to make them work for your group.

Generally age mixing in games can be positive if there's some way to remind adults that they don't have to "mark their territory" or prove anything by dominating the game or their team.

Sabbath Activity Twenty-one

The Welcome Pack

Theme and Rationale:
We often make passing, and perhaps well-intentioned, attempts at proclaiming how we welcome new members into our church families. We may have them stand, or we may mention their names as we sing another chorus of "I'm So Glad I'm a Part of the Family of God." It's not that we don't mean well, but the truth is that most of our caring in this issue allows the word "caring" to remain a noun and not a verb.

We all know that there's no loneliness like being lonely in a crowd. The creation of The Welcome Pack moves our talk from the ethereal, nebulous world of concepts to a more concrete reality. It forces us to deal with what the phrase "the church family" means.

Minimum Time Required:
An hour or more if there's been good preparation.

Preparation and Materials:
Brainstorm with others regarding resources of your church and community. Begin to collect a reservoir of supplies that specifically benefit someone new to your area. Local banks, real estate offices, and the chamber of commerce will often have items that are available for newcomers. Street maps are always helpful!

Many businesses and recreation parks offer discount coupons for goods and services in the hope of establishing friendships with new clientele. It wouldn't hurt if you specifically targeted the businesses and service organizations that operate by Christian principles.

If you have a local church school or academy, you may wish to ask if it would provide a supply of current bulletins or materials to go in your pack. Sometimes a school will even issue a coupon for something in

The Welcome Pack

order to encourage parents to commit to the Christian educational system.

You'll also need to provide some "blank checks" and pens for participants to make up some of their own items for the gift pack.

How To:

Have a room organized for the creation of the gift box. You'll provide boxes and stacks of the materials available for the package. You'll also need the "blank checks" to encourage members to make a specific commitment of friendship by writing in a skill or service they may offer. These could be such things as

"One free Sabbath dinner at our home—two weeks' notice, please."
"Three free hours of baby-sitting."
"Driveway cleared from snow one time—just call."
"I'll take your children to the zoo with mine. Let's plan it."
"A Friday evening at our home to welcome in Sabbath together."
"A special invitation to join our 'Girls' Night Out' crew."

It would be helpful to create two types of boxes, one for newly baptized members who have little or no background in our denomination and one for members who transfer in from another area. On any Sabbath that a new member family is welcomed, they can receive this gift box as an evidence of the truth that caring is a verb and not a noun.

You may wish to make a cassette tape while the box is being filled, as is done for the Adopt a Student Missionary activity. This personalizes the event and makes the new member feel more a part of the family.

How It Has Worked:

This is also a new idea for me, and I look forward to seeing it implemented somewhere. The whole concept appeals to me as being a solution to the dilemma of how we reach out to embrace the new ones of the flock.

By targeting specific issues in which we can offer our caring, we avoid the trap of saying, "If there's anything I can do for you, just give me a call." People never call on those terms, and if they did they might ask you to do something that you cannot do. Specific offers in the "blank checks" make you vulnerable, but they also free you to set the limits of how you can assist, and therefore you become vulnerable only in the areas in which you have gifts and a comfort zone.

Sabbath Activity Twenty-two

The Midrash Walk

Theme and Rationale:
Observant Jews have spent generations of Sabbaths by "making *midrash*." The term comes from two Hebrew concepts: *mi*—from, and *deresh*—teaching. Midrash is the art and exercise of equating two unrelated objects to learn and teach from the effort. Any leading idea opens up all forms of possibilities: "How is the law like an old overcoat?" "How is religion like my dog?" "How is morality like the Alps?"

Once a person gets into digging down into the midrash, new insights are gained. Often good ideas become exponential so that one concept and another don't just create two ideas, but a whole new spectrum of thoughts and challenges. Making midrash can be fun. It can also stretch your perceptions of what you believe and who you are.

In this exercise participants will be required to think of their life and where they feel they are at this time. It's a challenging activity and a pleasant way to spend some good Sabbath hours.

Minimum Time Required:
Not less than an hour.

Preparation and Materials:
This exercise takes very little preparation. All that's required is a space for the participants to wander out in nature and then a place where they can comfortably interact.

If you choose to have the group warm up to this, you'll have to prepare for that by providing the game, or music, or whatever tool you choose for the icebreaker period.

The Midrash Walk

How To:

It probably isn't best to start this exercise without some priming. Appropriate singing or a group interaction sheet could set the tone for what you're about to ask them to do. The object of this is to prepare a comfort zone and later be able to trust the group enough to become a bit vulnerable in the midrashic process.

After you feel you've appropriately set the stage for success in your activity, you'll divide the participants into small groups of not more than four or five. They'll be dismissed with very specific commands:

1. From this time until I call us back to order, I ask that none of you speak unless you're responding to this midrashic statement: "My life is like this _____ [some object in nature] because . . ."

2. You may choose more than one object with which to equate your life.

3. After 15 minutes you're to return to this area, again not speaking unless I ask you to. The only discussion for the next 15 minutes is to be statements that fulfill the midrash.

Then dismiss the group to make midrash. When they have returned, ask each person to share what another one said that was particularly meaningful.

You may then sense the mood to carry this on as long as you feel it's profitable. Any number of discussions can come from this, and with midrash you're never able to predetermine the flow of the stream. It finds its own level.

How It Has Worked:

This has been a provocative event for groups from teens on up. People gain incredible insights from the simple challenge of equating their lives to some struggling little bug, or some grass growing out of a hard place, or a tree being pulled in two directions. Get the idea?

FSA-5

Sabbath Activity Twenty-three

The *Shekel Shopper*

Theme and Rationale:
In the poem "Upon the Centennial Celebration," the writer shared his concern at looking back at the founding fathers and not really seeing them as living, breathing, sweating, vibrant people. He also spoke of the realization that when the bicentennial rolled around, people would not remember that his generation ate ripe apples, saw the colors of the fields, laughed, fell in love, and lived real lives. Do you perceive your parent's childhood as vividly as you remember your own?

It's fun and challenging to take the Bible characters and put real blood in their veins and real dirt on their sandals. The *Shekel Shopper* does that.

Minimum Time Required:
An hour or more.

Preparation and Materials:
You'll need to provide current copies of various classified ads or classified publications to inspire your group. It would probably be best to check to see if there are any sections you don't wish to make available, such as modeling, escort, massage, adult conversation, etc. (Who needs the hassle of having someone scan them or joke about them and break the mood?)

You'll also need to provide 3 x 5 or 4 x 6 note cards on which to write the ads. Each person (or cluster) will need at least 25.

This is the type of event during which you'll find that some good background music will set a nice tone for the work as it progresses.

The *Shekel Shopper*

How To:

After setting the appropriate tone for participation (by a song service or some other positive mixer), you'll explain the assignment. Your group is going to create the *Shekel Shopper*, the local classified ad paper that Moses or Paul or Jonah might have picked up when visiting the local King's Mart or chariot parts store. Esther or Peter might have scanned it when downing the cuisine at the local McDavid's. (By the way, in Jerusalem it really *is* called McDavid's!)

Divide your group into clusters of ad writers—groups of not more than three people. Give each cluster a sample sheet of modern classified ads, and then assign them to write at least one classified for an Old Testament character and at least one for a New Testament character in each of the following classifications

    Transportation
    Real Estate
    Farm Equipment
    Items for Sale
    Lost and Found
    Musical Instruments
    Business Opportunities
    Employment
    Livestock, Pets, and Produce
    Miscellaneous Services
    Personals
    Birth Notices
    Death Notices

Put on some nice background music, and let the creative juices flow. At the conclusion of the time allotted, arrange the ads by category and display them on a bulletin board where everyone can enjoy the work of others for a while.

How It Has Worked:

Each time I've allowed people to put the biblical episodes into modern context I've found that they really enjoy the challenge and usually come up with many creative ideas. Also the atmosphere of creativity sparks even greater creativity.

Many will not stop at two for each category but will continue on just because they're having fun.

Sabbath Activity Twenty-four

City Planners

Theme and Rationale:

According to a common interpretation of 1 Corinthians 2:9, heaven will be better than we can think or dream. (The context indicates that Paul was describing God's saving acts and not the future life in eternity.) I've often told groups around the world to dream big and to dream lavishly when they think of heaven, because it paints God into a corner! If you think of only harps and clouds and the generic picture of heaven, then God doesn't have to do much to improve on what you believe. If you wish to have a plain vanilla heaven, that's up to you, but I prefer to dream big. I prefer to let my imagination run uncontrolled when it comes to the possibilities of what heaven will be like, and then I know it has to be better than that for God to fulfill His word.

This City Planners activity allows for big dreams and wild imagination. It also makes this present reality pale in comparison.

Minimum Time Required:

Usually not less than two hours.

Preparation and Materials:

You'll need to determine the approximate number of participants and divide that number so that you'll end up with groups of not more than five or six people. Each group should be provided with at least five white poster board sheets, pencils, crayons or colored pencils, rulers, geometric design items, a compass—whatever materials you feel would be beneficial in their planning and execution of their city design.

It would probably be best if each group had a table and enough space to work without being crowded, distracted, or disturbed.

City Planners

How To:

Divide your crew into working teams of not more than five or six people. Read them 1 Corinthians 2:9, and tell them that they have the privilege of designing the New Jerusalem. They're the city planning team that will serve as consultants for Jesus as He is working to prepare a place for His people (John 14:1-3).

They'll have a four-part assignment and will need to determine how they'll fulfill all four segments. It will be up to them to either brainstorm one part and then assign its fulfillment to a member or two or let all the team members have a hand in each segment. (The first option is probably more efficient.)

One piece of poster board should list all public buildings in the city. It should briefly describe the building and its purpose.

One piece of poster board should display any theme parks or recreation areas. What happens in each one? Why does it exist?

One piece of poster board should show any temples, shrines, or sacred spots. Are there any special memorial sites?

The last piece of poster board should show the general layout (from an aerial view) of the city itself. It will show all locations of mansion neighborhoods. Other items required are the site of God's throne, the river of life and tree of life, the sea of glass. All items from segments 1, 2, and 3 should be shown on this general map also.

Remind the participants that this isn't about art but about creativity.

How It Has Worked:

This has always been a challenging and enjoyable exercise for every group over the age of 10 or so that I've tried it with.

I'll not forget the time that Mindy Wagner taught me that the city will be divided into four quadrants—the spring, the summer, the fall, and the winter sections. She wanted a place where all four seasons were available at any given time.

I say to Mindy and to all, "Dream on!"

Sabbath Activity Twenty-five

The Great Prophecy Clip

Theme and Rationale:
   Usually we're wrapped up in the nuts and bolts of daily living. We often fall into the old forest-and-trees syndrome because of the demands of daily life. Once in a while it's healthy to get a larger picture of where we are and where we are going. (When I stop to look at the $13 watch on my wrist, I realize that 10 years ago the richest king couldn't have owned it!) The explosion of technology is astounding. Knowledge is surely being increased.
   This activity can also teach that it's infinitely more important to know how to avoid the disease than to just become an expert on the disease itself. It will be little consolation in hell to say that you had the most intricate time-line chart in all the church. The Great Prophecy Clip exercise gives time for a larger perspective on where we are and what's really important to us.

Minimum Time Required:
   Probably an hour or more.

Preparation and Materials:
   You'll need to collect a large variety of recent magazines and newspapers. (Plan to have a sufficient number so that each participant will have at least one newspaper and one magazine.) You'll also need poster board or scrapbook pages, scissors, and rubber cement with relatively easy access for each participant. You'll need space that allows a person to spread out to work in a comfortable zone. This activity would be enhanced with appropriate background music as the exercise proceeds.

The Great Prophecy Clip

How To:

First spend some time talking about the prophetic mind-set. Explain how very few people in Christianity were really geared toward discussions of the end-time or prophetic fulfillment until the late 1960s. When Hal Lindsey wrote *The Late Great Planet Earth,* it seemed to give mainstream Christianity permission to get really involved in eschatological concerns, and suddenly Seventh-day Adventists didn't stand alone in the field anymore.

Discuss the typical things that are quoted when believers begin to list signs of the end, and then provide time for the fulfillment of the following assignment.

Participants are to take at least one newspaper and one magazine, from which they are to cut out every article, advertisement, headline, or picture that wouldn't have been in a magazine or newspaper in 1965. (Have it focused on the idea, technology, concept, or issue, and not just on individuals. It's obvious that Bill Clinton wouldn't have made the headlines in 1965.)

As they compile their representative pieces let them put them into some group composite of a bulletin board or a scrapbook.

When the allotted time has been completed, have a discussion concerning the experience. Two great leading questions are

1. What did you find that you didn't expect?
2. How do you feel about what you've done and seen?

A good shift in the discussion then would be to talk about what's more important—knowing the disease really well or understanding the preventative or antidote?

Many Christians fall into the trap of focusing on the sensational and specific details of prophetic time lines. The larger issue is knowing how to be in God's hands when it all falls. Understanding why the third toenail of the fourth beast of Revelation 11 is painted green won't save anybody. It's more important to know how not to get the mark of the beast than to be able to define what it is.

How It Has Worked:

This is a healthy reminder activity. It has always challenged, at least for a time, the complacency of the groups. But it serves no purpose without the ending focus on what our priorities should be even if Christ doesn't come for 10,000 years. After all, some are going through their time of trouble now and won't even be part of the equation when the real thing hits.

Sabbath Activity Twenty-six

Performing Tashlik

Theme and Rationale:

There's real strength in finding concrete ways to enact what you choose to believe in your life. Psychologists know full well that it's terribly important for a person to reinforce good intentions and healthy choices by acting upon them in measurable, concrete ways.

At the time of the reevaluation of life just prior to Yom Kippur (Day of Atonement), Jews have found a very healing, positive means to enact good choices regarding God's forgiveness and self-forgiveness. This is accomplished by the performance of tashlik.

This ritual is a psychologically strong enactment of decisions and choices. Christians would do well to incorporate something like this into their own lives and spiritual rituals.

Minimum Time Required:

Not less than an hour.

Preparation and Materials:

A good amount of bread—preferably old, hard, and a bit stale—in individual bags.

You'll also need a location that your group can walk to that is a site of "living water." It must be flowing water and not a pond or lake. It cannot be the ocean, because it has current action that comes and goes. The water source for tashlik must have a flow that goes in one direction—downstream, away from you.

How To:

Though done in a group, this is a very personal and private exercise. It can be a therapeutic and healing event if done appropriately.

Performing Tashlik

First explain what tashlik is. Explain that it's a chance to review the past, acknowledge the pain of personal failures and the grief received because of the failures of others.

Give each person in your group a small bag of old bread and have a location where they spend at least 10 to 15 minutes walking. As the group is walking you may wish to sing in order to keep the mood appropriate for what they are about to do.

Upon arrival at the location ask each person to find his or her own individual spot for his or her tashlik. Everyone should remain within sight but with private space.

Tell them that they'll have about 20 minutes to do this in any prayerful method that they choose.

They should
1. Think of a specific failure of their life.
2. Tear off a small piece of bread to represent that failure.
3. Cast the bread into the water as an enactment of surrender of that failure.
4. Watch as God's stream takes it away.

By this act they forgive themselves for what they've done, shouldn't have done, or should have done but neglected to do. They may use the same procedure for specific failures of others who have hurt them. This is more than an enactment of self-forgiveness. It assists in relieving the resentments that bind them. Without an act like this the offender will forever have "free rent in their head," and the offense will continue. The offender's power is released by choosing to walk out from under it by casting it away.

At the conclusion gather the group together for responding to the act, offering prayer, and maybe participating in a Communion service.

How It Has Worked:

This is a really healing act. When performed well, it allows me to live in forgiveness and acceptance.

A lovely young lady came to me one evening after I spoke at the Washington Conference camp meeting. She'd had a history of heinous sexual abuse at the hand of her father. I urged her to try tashlik.

A few mornings later I saw her walking up from the river with an empty plastic bag. I asked her how it went, and she replied, "This is the first time I've smiled in years."

The Lord was right—casting bread on waters does bring rich returns.

Sabbath Activity Twenty-seven

Bible Boggle

Theme and Rationale:
This is another game that not only provides opportunity to use Bible knowledge in an entertaining way but also enhances fellowship and participation.

Because of the specific design of the game, it can be used without threat in a group in which some have a great deal of Bible background and others are limited in their confidence. Usually the Bible "hotshot" will either be considerate of those who have less of a reservoir of Bible trivia or will try to impress everyone with his or her ability to dig up the difficult stuff. Regardless, this game offers less knowledgeable Bible students an opportunity to deal on the level that they know and not be shut out.

We are hardly saved by this type of activity, but it may keep some who waver near the Source because they enjoy the activities.

Minimum Time Required:
An hour or more.

Preparation and Materials:
Plan to provide a good amount of scrap paper and writing instruments.
For timing you might have a background CD and utilize the length of several songs as the amount of time for each round.

How To:
Have the group divide into a number of teams (probably not more than four). Ask them to mix themselves so that each team has a fair representation of "Bible scholars" and "Bible novices."

Then tell them that their group has the length of two songs to compile the largest list that they can in the assigned category (for instance, "The

Bible Boggle

Miracles of Jesus").

When the two songs are concluded, ask the first team to read out all the miracles that they came up with. If any other group listed the same miracle, both teams must scratch that off the list. They will receive credit only for the miracles that they have come up with that no one else has listed.

When the first group has finished their list, the next group reads theirs, using the same process. Then move on to the next, etc. When the last group's turn comes around, they must read their list just so that it can be heard. By that point there should be no duplications.

Each group gets 10 points for every item that they came up with that wasn't duplicated by another group. Any answer may be challenged, and if it's determined from Scripture that it was an invalid answer, the team loses 30 points. The moderator renders the final judgment in this.

Then move on to another round in which another category is given, and continue the process.

Some other suggested categories include Bible animals; prophets; kings and queens; Bible cities; specific Bible women; New Testament churches; questions asked in the Bible; holidays, celebrations, and holy days; items related to the sanctuary; parables; Bible plagues and disasters; Bible battles; specific prayers in the Bible.

How It Has Worked:

This has been fun, challenging, and nonthreatening. Even those who normally sit on their hands often get drawn into participation, because they usually have something to contribute.

Fellowship is worth something, isn't it?

Sabbath Activity Twenty-eight

Aunt Tillie's Gift

Theme and Rationale:
We would do well to randomly ask ourselves questions like
   What things make a church viable?
   How much should we spend on facilities?
   How much should we allocate to programs?
   How much should we invest in people?

We may serve a God who is limitless, but so far the church faces the same financial realities as does any other organization on earth. Our human and financial resources seem to be limited. These realities force the church board to prioritize from the pool of available funds.

This is a very simple exercise that provides an interesting forum for people to challenge themselves about what they hold of value in their church and where their value system would invest the resources. By doing this we eventually come to the ultimate question "What really is the church?"

Minimum Time Required:
Usually not less than an hour.

Preparation and Materials:
A comfortable location for the participants to break into small groups and nice background music to enhance the working atmosphere.

How To:
Divide the participants into small working groups. It's advantageous to encourage husbands and wives or family units not to be in the same group in situations like this. (Often the living structure of their established relationships will so quickly come into play that some who might actively

Aunt Tillie's Gift

participate get shut out. The husband has to dominate the wife, or the kids just want to argue with Mom, or one family member fades into the background because that's the common dynamic in the home. It's just best not to predispose your groups to some rut because of the unspoken, understood roles of expectation that develop in almost every home.)

Explain the following:

"Dear old Aunt Tillie, a faithful member of the church family, recently passed away. We'll miss her sitting on the seventh row over there on the left side. We'll miss the stable assurance of her strong 'Amen' whenever the pastor makes any reference to the responsibilities of husbands and fathers.

"The mural she put up on the junior room wall back in the 1940s is now quite faded. It never was great art, but it was a labor of love, and no one wanted to touch it while she was alive. (Now everyone wonders who will be the first to say that maybe we should paint over it. After all, she hasn't been dead very long.)

"Her favorite hymn won't be sung the same, and a few people will miss the dubious casserole of string beans and some excuse of gravy and meat substitute stuff that she brought to every potluck every Sabbath since 1844. (She was always a little hurt if at least one person didn't ask her for the recipe so that she could say, 'Oh, it's just something that I throw together out of my head.')

"She was a quirky old lady, but basically sweet and harmless.

"Well, they just read her will, and to everyone's surprise she left $15,000 as an unrestricted gift to the church family. We can do anything we want with it. How are we going to spend it?"

Then allow the teams to run the gamut. Unless there's an absolute, universally agreed upon, pressing need in your church family, this raises a lot of really amazing issues. Unless your heat system is completely dead, you'll find a lot of values will be portrayed in the discussions as they progress. Eventually bring it all back to the larger group.

How It Has Worked:

It's always amazing. Some want to invest in stained glass, others in carpet, and don't forget missions! Some want to give 15 people $1,000 each to produce something for building up the kingdom.

This exercise really challenges what we think the church should be. It really works!

Sabbath Activity Twenty-nine

Creation Texture Boxes

Theme and Rationale:
Those of us who have the privilege of being sighted can hardly comprehend blindness. How would you describe the sunset to someone who's never even seen his or her mother's face? What is red to a person who's never looked at a hand?

Creation Texture Boxes is an exercise that gives benefits twice: (1) it challenges and educates those who make them, and (2) it blesses those who receive the gift.

Minimum Time Required:
This would be best as a full Sabbath event if the first part was tackled Friday evening, and the Creation portion done during Sabbath afternoon.

Preparation and Materials:
A good relationship must be established with an organization that works with and for the sight-impaired people in your community. If you don't know of a local school or a center with resources for the visually impaired, you may have to start from scratch. Calling a local governmental agency that assists in social services might be your first contact point. Someone there should be able to direct you to local resources.

Once you find the agencies that assist the visually impaired, explain what you wish to do, and let the agency assist you in creating the logistics for the event. This may take some negotiation, because while you might feel that something would be wonderful, their experience will give helpful guidance as to what truly would be mutually beneficial.

Let your expert friends share whatever they deem most helpful as you set up your location for the event.

You'll need to provide at least one set of seven solid shoe boxes. The

Creation Texture Boxes

number of sets will be determined by the number of participants you expect and how many people you wish to involve as a creative team for each set.

How To:

Allow a predetermined period of time for the education/awareness phase of the agenda. Some of the planned segments could include sharing, interaction, and then a question-and-answer section with one or more visually impaired people, instructors for the visually impaired, service dog trainers, or government officials who work with the sight-impaired. The guests could suggest various activities to allow the sighted to better understand the challenges of blindness. You may even want your group to take guided trust walks.

Before you conclude the first section, share with the participants what they'll be participating in for the conclusion of the event. (Having a period of time between the two sections allows for some brainstorming and consideration as to how one might fulfill the second phase.)

The last part of the event is geared to creating a meaningful gift for the visually impaired based on the seven days of Creation. Box 1 should be a sensory creation to help the visually impaired understand light. Box 2 will be a hands-on creation to represent the separation of the firmament. Box 3 will contrast dryness and wetness in a lasting form. And you continue on through the Creation week experience.

Set a specific time for the completion of the project, and then let the groups attack it. Materials for this are limited only by the imagination of the participants.

When all groups have completed their tasks, you should have a rather remarkable gift to present to someone who will really appreciate it.

How It Has Worked:

I've used this as a part of a series on various physical handicaps and challenges. It's provided a good interaction and really stretches the creativity of those who have had their eyes opened by considering blindness. Sabbath thus has become an opportunity to be blessed and to bless.

Sabbath Activity Thirty

The Heritage Video

Theme and Rationale:
Selfishness is bringing great shifts within our society. The mass population of the baby boom years is no longer young. As a result, advertisers no longer use only 22-year-old California beach bunnies to sell products. There's a very evident growing proliferation of young-looking-edging-on-grayness models, showing that they live rich and vibrant lives with this phone service or that low-fat butter substitute.

Madison Avenue may be manipulative but certainly not stupid. The largest proportion of the American population is now 34 to 52 years old, and it's not getting any younger.

The church faces the same reality. The graying of the church is evident in almost every congregation and certainly at every old style effort (such as camp meetings).

If time lasts, we're going to be forced to honor and value the older generation, because for most of us it will be us!

We have too long not cherished the incredible treasure and resource of those who have earned maturity. We've not taken from them what they have to give. Old age has been a disease to quarantine.

The universal fear of the aged is abandonment. If you're old, every day brings you the awareness that fewer and fewer of your friends are alive. Too often those who still have a life to live are too busy to include you in theirs. That defines abandonment.

The Heritage Video exercise is an interesting way to address this problem with a healthy intergenerational activity.

Minimum Time Required:
At least one afternoon.

The Heritage Video

Preparation and Materials:
This depends on the size of your group and how many portions you wish to create for the activity. Your menu for this will be determined by how elaborate you wish to make it, and whether you want to include a meal or banquet as part of the conclusion. The bare minimum will be having an available video camera and solid arrangements with the "stars" of your video.

How To:
First spend time with your group, opening up the general issues of aging. Then allow your group to design the style of the video. It can be done as a news broadcast, a person-in-the-street interview, a docudrama, a composite, a group retrospective with several people at once—any format they wish. (Stress that the better the planning, the less sloppiness they'll regret that they won't be able to undo by editing.) Well-prepared segments produce much better results.

It would be most valuable if the video focused on important issues—history and feelings. A general "How are you today?" will cheat the elderly of really sharing something of quality, and it will bore your group to tears. You have to deal with feelings and memories to allow these precious "resources" to give what they have to offer. Plan to let their individual personalities shine. Let them teach what they have to share.

Short segments will be more challenging and more productive. Incessant droning will put everyone to sleep, both young and old.

The group or groups will then go to keep the appointment made with those who are going to be the focus of their program. It's imperative that previous arrangements have been made for this. It would be rude not to do so.

You may wish to conclude the event with a vespers meal and "screening" or save it for a later time in a worship service.

Wouldn't it be meaningful for your pastor to have a library of these precious memories to show at an inevitable funeral six months or two years later? That concept raises a lot of positive issues of life, gratitude for a good life, and hope for a resurrection when old Uncle Walter will be raised to be 23 years old forever.

How It Has Worked:
This is a new thought for me that has grown from the concern of the graying of the church. I've not yet had an opportunity to implement it, but I see it as having great possibilities.

Perhaps you can try it before I do and let me know how it can be adapted to be really magnificent.

FSA-6

Sabbath Activity Thirty-one

Bible Baseball

Theme and Rationale:
This activity provides another opportunity to use the stories, facts, and trivia of the Scriptures in a positive way. Because of the design of the game, it doesn't hold as much potential threat to those who feel that they might make fools of themselves.

Because the participants create half the game themselves, it also challenges them to deal with broader general Bible knowledge than the few questions that they'll have to answer themselves. The style of the game easily involves all and keeps them involved.

Let me stress again that Bible trivia isn't what salvation is all about, but feeling positively about dealing with spiritual issues isn't a bad contribution. Sometimes the games can serve as a tool to keep people close until the correct catalyst of events allows for conviction and conversion to real religion.

Admittedly Bible Baseball isn't the meat, but it's comfortable for those who aren't ready for meat yet. Perhaps the day will come when they won't choke on deeper Scripture involvement than games.

Minimum Time Required:
Probably two hours.

Preparation and Materials:
A comfortable room or outdoor location. Four chairs should be positioned at the front in a baseball diamond pattern. Scratch paper for two teams and arrangements for two neutral, mature team captains.

How To:
Divide your group into two relatively equal teams (size and abilities

Bible Baseball

in Bible knowledge). Assign one neutral team captain to assist in keeping the team focused and predisposed to being fair in their part of the creation of the game.

Give a set amount of time (probably an hour) for the teams to create 50 sets of four "pitches." A set consists of four Bible questions related to one person, place, thing, category, or theme. The questions start with a fairly simple question and progress in difficulty to the fourth question, which should be challenging but not impossible.

Example: Category—Noah
1. How long did it rain during the Flood?
2. How did Noah try to find out if the water had receded?
3. Give the specific names of three people in the ark.
4. How old was Noah when the flood came?

Your team captain will help enforce the one rule for the questions: No question may be used as a "pitch" unless someone in the team creating those questions knows the answer without looking it up in the Bible. That gives hope that someone on the other team has a chance to get it.

When the allocated time is up, call the teams together to play the game. Start with one team and call up the first person, who sits at the "home base" chair. The opposing team captain states the category, and asks if the "batter" wishes to go for a single, double, triple, or home run. If the "hitter" asks for a double, he or she has to answer question 2 in that category. If he or she gets it right, he or she goes to the "second base" chair. If the question is missed, it becomes the first out of the inning. (The same is true for singles, triples, and home runs.)

Players are "forced" around the chairs by their teammates, and runs are counted when players get back to the "home base" chair.

If there are fewer than two outs and "runners" on base and a "batter" misses the question (no matter what the value), a base runner can say, "I want to steal" if he or she knows the answer. If the base runner's answer is correct, he or she advances one base (and forces anyone ahead to move along also). If wrong, he or she also makes an out and has to sit with the rest of the team.

After three outs the other team is up to bat, and the process continues with the opposing captain now reading the questions. (Categories are to be taken in order and not tailor-made for a specific batter.)

How It Has Worked:

This has proven many times to afford good, clean Bible fun and fellowship for all ages.

Sabbath Activity Thirty-two

The Hezekiah Tree

Theme and Rationale:

I'm not completely naive. This activity has the potential to raise the hackles of some saints. It definitely breaks the agricultural prohibition of the Mishnah, but it opens up all kinds of interaction from a simple Scripture enactment.

Planting a tree is a statement of faith, a symbolic participation in Creation, a reminder of many Bible stories, an opening to discuss God's deliverance, an action that reminds us of our dominion of the earth, and a proactive choice for environmental stewardship.

Those who manage the funds for the Society for the Reforestation of Israel allow individuals to establish a memorial by the planting of a tree, a grove, or a forest in one's own name (or someone else's whom you would wish to honor). It's seen as a prophetic fulfillment. The participants are seen to be assisting in bringing about the age of the Messiah, because they'll begin to cause "the desert [to] . . . blossom as the rose" (Isa. 35:1).

At the official Holocaust memorial in Jerusalem, Yad Vashem, along the Avenue of the Righteous, trees are planted in honor of those righteous Gentiles who risked their lives as rescuers.

Planting a tree can be a sacred act.

The rabbis have often said: "If you are planting a tree when Messiah appears, finish planting the tree, then go out to greet Him. He will understand."

Minimum Time Required:

Depending on how much substance you put into it, this could take several hours and would be well worth the investment!

The Hezekiah Tree

Preparation and Materials:

Purchase a tree or trees, obtain materials and tools for planting, and get permission for the location of the planting.

You should create a study assignment appropriately geared to your group from the following passages: Genesis 3:1-19; 18:1-8; Judges 9:7-15; 1 Kings 19:4-8; 2 Kings 19:31-34; Psalm 1:3; Isaiah 35:1; 55:12, 13; Matthew 12:33; Revelation 22:1-3. The assignment could include enacted parables, having one group teach the other about the lessons from their assigned passage or passages. (Psalm 1:3 alone provides a ton of concepts. I ought to know—in 1980 it was my inspiration for a whole book, *He Shall Be Like a Tree*.)

Without surrendering the secret of what you plan to do, you should warn your participants that they might get dirty and should come dressed accordingly.

How To:

Break the group into teams of not more than four or five. Give them your Scripture assignments, and then allow them time to fulfill them. At the end of the Scripture segment, spend time discussing what concepts they've learned and what new thoughts have struck them.

I think focusing particularly on the Hezekiah story (with Rabshakeh's mythical offer to provide them with a home and fruit if they would abandon their confidence in God's deliverance and how God told them to plant and plan to eat from what they planted) is a challenging precursor to this event. Do we really trust God to pull this off, or are we willing to run after offered substitutes?

The actual tree planting then can be a service of recommitment, prayer, and worship. Would I go out and do the actual planting at that time, still on Sabbath? With this solid preparation you bet I would! It could be an incredibly sacred exercise. The tree or trees planted would be a living reminder to all who participate.

How It Has Worked:

I've done the tree study, and it's been really positive, but I've only recently considered the next step of actually enacting the commitment by group planting. I'm looking forward to trying this.

Sabbath Activity Thirty-three

The Revelation Relief

Theme and Rationale:
What passage of Scripture provides more opportunity for creative imagination than the book of Revelation? Each chapter contains so much graphic symbolism and every description is so challenging that they both invite—and defy—portrayal. But that's another reason for gratitude. God allows us to let our imaginations run, and creative juices can really flow when we open the pages of John's apocalypse.

The Revelation Relief exercise gives an opportunity both to those who are particularly gifted in artistic abilities and the rest of us who aren't able to tackle those images.

Minimum Time Required:
Probably at least an hour, not including the time for baking.

Preparation and Materials:
You'll need to provide enough creative dough for 22 panels and 22 disposable pie pans. Here's the recipe:

> 4 cups white flour
> 3 cups salt
> 1½ cups water

Mix salt and flour. Add water, and knead seven to 10 minutes until very smooth. Divide the mixture into two equal parts and put them in plastic wrap. The mixture will stay fresh in the refrigerator for up to five days.

If making the dough requires too much commitment of time or energy, you can substitute by purchasing modeling clay from a craft store. Children's Play-Doh modeling clay can also be purchased if you wish to

The Revelation Relief

make the end result somewhat more colorful, but I think less dignified.

You'll need table space for messy creativity by a group of your size. Music always provides a nice background for this type of activity.

How To:

Divide your group into units that will be able to produce 22 relief panels. Then assign each segment of your group the chapter/chapters that they'll have for their panel. After reviewing the assigned chapter, a representative symbolism is chosen for that chapter.

Some possibilities from Revelation 1 might be an island, an angel, seven stars, a crown, a throne, a lampstand, a sword, keys, or any combination of those items. Each chapter provides many creative opportunities.

After five or 10 minutes to allow the motif for each chapter to be chosen, distribute two clusters of dough for each chapter. A base for the relief is created by packing one ball of dough in the lightly oiled pie pan.

Then the rest of the dough is used to create the chosen image or images on the base. The end result will be an artistic relief that should clearly show a symbol for the theme of the assigned chapter.

The panels are baked at 275° to 300° F from 40 minutes to up to two hours, depending on the thickness of the pattern. (To give a nice antique brown sheen to the panel, brush mayonnaise on the surface after baking for 15 or 20 minutes.)

You'll have 22 panels to hang on some display wall when the task is completed.

How It Has Worked:

This is fun, and I'm always amazed at the imagination that gets released when the correct atmosphere is created.

Sabbath Activity Thirty-four

Bible Actionary

Theme and Rationale:
Playing Bible games, as stated before, can often degenerate into being simple time fillers. In some ways that's as offensive as taking the Bible itself and using it as a simple paper weight. The Scriptures are not to be just utilitarian.

But if the "trivia" can be utilized to enhance the enjoyment of God's Word, challenge creativity, and encourage healthy interaction and fellowship, then I feel the games have a purpose that would not at all displease the Lord.

Bible Actionary is one of the best I've used.

Minimum Time Required:
Probably at least an hour.

Preparation and Materials:
You'll need two dice (one red and one white) and a coin.

You'll also need to create 15 or 20 clues in six categories:
- Old Testament People (for example, Joseph, Isaac, Jael, Haman)
- New Testament People (for instance, Eutychus, Peter, Dorcas, Martha)
- Old Testament Places and Things (such as whale, Jericho, Eden)
- New Testament Places and Things (that is, Rome, armor, synagogue)
- Potluck (any of the above)
- Bible Concepts (for instance, sin, grace, hope, evil, forgiveness, miracle)

Bible Actionary

You'll need to plan to have a song leader who is capable of getting the group involved in singing as each round is being prepared by the chosen participants.

How To:

Divide the group into three teams of equal size, abilities, and gregariousness. (Don't let all the shy ones end up on the same team.)

Explain that they'll roll the two dice together and then flip the coin.

The coin will determine if the Actionary will be performed only for their team (heads) or for anyone from any team to guess (tails). The dice will determine the category (red and number) as well as the number of people involved in the skit/action/enactment (white and number).

Example: A three on the red die means that the next word from the "Old Testament Place or Thing" will be the assignment. A four on the white means that the person who rolled the die will choose three others to join him or her in acting—a total of four people. (If you have teams of fewer than seven, they'll have to select people from some of the other teams.)

When the category and people to perform in the skit are determined, they're sent away to another room (or other close location if you're doing this outdoors) to prepare for the enactment. They have only the length of one song (or two short ones) to prepare.

The song leader then gets the remaining participants to join in singing. When the music is over, the group returns and acts out the word or concept for the whole group. (The coin will determine if anyone can guess or if it's limited to the team that rolled the dice.)

The Actionary is to be completely a charade—no sounds or props are to assist in the portrayal.

Whoever guesses the *exact* word or words correctly will earn a point for their team and then will roll the dice for the next round.

The game ends when you've run out of words for one category.

How It Has Worked:

This has been an excellent intergenerational game. People of all ages enjoy it, and it forces broad-spectrum participation. Because people get "drafted" or "forced" to act with the one who rolls the dice, it's not easy for a person to sit by uninvolved.

Watching the imaginative presentations and being drawn to guess the word or concept are magnetic. I've not seen this fail in a group yet.

Sabbath Activity Thirty-five

Challah and Love Loaves

Theme and Rationale:

Back in the old days when making bread was an everyday life reality this activity would probably have fallen into the category of common work. But modern living now renders breadmaking a therapeutic (and aromatic) teaching event.

Challah is the knotted bread made by observant Jews to celebrate the entrance of the Sabbath Queen on Friday evening. No particular recipe is required. It doesn't have to be unleavened, and even cinnamon rolls can be utilized. Throw in some raisins if it makes you happy!

The braiding or knotting of the dough is a weekly reminder of the belief that Israel is bound to God by the covenant. You have to choose to be chosen. In Genesis 22 Isaac was symbolically bound on the altar as a vicarious representative of all Israel choosing to be bound. Generations of faithful Jews have called this event by the Hebrew term for binding—the *Akedah*.

Our Lord was born in Bethlehem, "the house of bread." He must have had an obvious purpose when He called Himself "the bread of life." In the memorial ritual He established for His children before His death, Jesus equated His very existence to bread.

Twelve sacred loaves graced the golden table on the north side of the holy place.

So much about bread is violent. From harvest to eating, the whole process of breadmaking is violent.

There's something sacred about hands working good, clean, moist dough. There's a special sensory blessing in the aroma of fresh bread. Weren't we told a long time ago that "there is more religion in a loaf of good bread than many think" (Ellen G. White, *The Ministry of Healing*, p. 302)?

Now do you see promise in a group afternoon of *challah* baking?

Challah and Love Loaves

Minimum Time Required:
Probably at least half an hour is needed to consider some of the scriptural issues raised above and then at least an hour, not counting the baking time.

Preparation and Materials:
You'll need to have several proven recipes and enough ingredients for your participants to enjoy taking part in the activity. Obviously they'll need table space, and eventually there needs to be an arrangement to bake the amount made.

You may wish to have access to a good book on *challah* to inspire everyone with artistic possibilities. One of the best on this is *Hallah*, by Malkah Drucker.

If you aren't a bread baker yourself, you may wish to draft an expert, who can pleasantly encourage and assist. Good music will enhance this activity.

How To:
Spend time setting the tone for the event by discussing some of the spiritual issues about bread in the Bible. You may wish to ask each participant to come up with more lessons and analogies as he or she works on the bread.

Show the representative pictures of some *challah* that has been created, and then let your teams have a try at it.

After the bread is completed, you may wish to provide an opportunity for it to be shared in a "loaf love meal." The bread itself will almost be enough for this. Perhaps a little margarine and jam would top it off wonderfully.

A retirement center or nursing home might be an appropriate forum for sharing the "love loaf meal." Your participants will even be forced to interact and answer questions about why the bread looks so strange.

How It Has Worked:
A lot of good things come out of this—sensory blessings, spiritual insights, appreciation for the art, and intergenerational interaction. There really is a lot of religion in a loaf of good bread!

Sabbath Activity Thirty-six

Sand Painting

Theme and Rationale:
Religious symbolism, well portrayed, can evoke a deep stirring in the heart of the believer. It almost seems ingrained for us to sense a response from the rich resonance of a pipe organ, the odor and texture of fresh leather on the cover of a new Bible, or the variegated shadows from a stained-glass window pouring across dark pews.

We deprive ourselves of an opportunity for spiritual wonder if we completely surrender those old anchors.

Minimum Time Required:
To be done well this could take several hours.

Preparation and Materials:
You'll need to have sufficient quantities of the following materials for your group:

Sheets of sandpaper—probably at least four sheets per person. (I prefer the black or gray sandpaper to the tan or orange.)

Inexpensive (with emphasis on the cheap part of it!) one-eighth-inch watercolor paintbrushes. Craft stores have these in bulk. (They should be throwaways.)

White craft glue. (You'll probably find that this works better if it's watered down a bit—not too much, though.)

A variety of colored sand. Some people spray paint their own sand in a paper bag and shake it around. I think this is much more effort than it's worth. It's messy, and you waste a lot of sand and paint. At craft stores you can purchase sand in about 10 different colors. It doesn't cost much, and you need such a small amount for each project that I feel it's best to purchase it. You'll have enough sand to do this several times (un-

Sand Painting

less you're working with a group of a thousand).

A supply of rulers, compasses, protractors, pencils, carbon paper, etc.

This can be more colorful (although a little bit more messy) if done with felt squares as a base of the design instead of sheets of sandpaper.

How To:

Let participants choose a combination of simple designs from the heritage symbols of Judeo-Christianity—a cross, a menorah, a dove, a Star of David, a Bible, a scroll, an angel, etc.

Then they design a workable, attractive mural using four base sheets as the background. Once they finish the design, they may draw out their full-sized prototype on scratch paper.

When the working model is satisfactory, it is transferred (by using carbon paper) onto the base material. Then the base material should be put on a sheet of newspaper (to capture and recycle the loose sand that gets painted on).

After choosing one color of sand, they're to put a light coat of glue on the appropriate spaces that coincide with that color, one space at a time. While the space is still wet, the appropriate color of sand is poured onto the wet glue. Then they move on to other spaces that need the same color.

When all the red, or blue, or whatever is sprinkled onto the pictures, they turn the pattern on edge so that the loose sand falls onto the newspaper. This is how the excess (and most of it will be excess) is recovered for further use.

Moving on through the other colors, the participants complete their murals.

Care should be taken to keep the various colors of sand "pure," as they can easily be polluted by not allowing previous colors to really set or dry before moving on to others. One method to avoid this is to move from the lighter colors to the darker, because the amount of intermingling is minimized when working in that order.

When completed, this artwork can be framed, hung, or displayed in any format that the participants find attractive.

How It Has Worked:

This has been a good craft-type project for anyone from ages 9 or so on up. Anyone younger than that usually needs assistance, unless you don't mind things a bit messy and a lot of sand being adulterated and lost.

I've seen some beautiful creations come out of this activity, and even people who tend to fear attempting fine art usually enjoy working in this medium.

Sabbath Activity Thirty-seven

The Conflict Mirror

Theme and Rationale:
We're all limited in our abilities. My brother chairs the math department at a university, and the last math class I ever took was Algebra I in high school. (I got twice as much out of it as he did, because I took one year's worth in two!)

One of the guaranteed limitations we all struggle against is our inability to see issues and life from the perspective of another. It's a rare person who really has developed this particular skill.

Experts in conflict resolution have taught us that the first step for reconciliation is for two people to at least come to acknowledge the right of the other party to have his or her feelings and perspective. We may not understand or agree with those feelings and that point of view, but at least we need to affirm that the other person feels the way he or she does. Then we can move on to resolution.

The Conflict Mirror deals with these issues.

Minimum Time Required:
Probably at least an hour.

Preparation and Materials:
Very little is needed for this event except to try to encourage participation by groups that have some diversity. Try to utilize this when you can have some parents mixed with their children, husbands and wives, unmarried males and females, or groups that show real racial and ethnic diversity. Other than that you'll need a balanced, positive moderator.

How To:
First begin the exercise with your target groups intermingled. Try not

The Conflict Mirror

to allow the separation factors to dominate the event from the beginning. Your best hope for finding real unity and mutual understandings won't come by starting with an understood line of demarcation.

After you've begun with some singing and other mixer-type games or activities, split the group into its two natural divisions (parents and kids, husbands and wives, etc.). The moderator will ask leading questions that set the tone for the event. These questions must be very specific. They should come from perception and not accusation. You can really shoot yourself in the foot if you come at this from the wrong angle. Here are some examples:

"Good Questions"	"Ouch!"
"Husbands, what do you think wives generally want?"	"Men, what is it about women that you don't understand?"
"What do you think it's like to be a racial minority?"	"Why do you think minority students are so sensitive?"
"How do you think your parents feel about _____?"	"What is it about your kids that drives you nuts?"

After perceptions have been aired, parents are now assigned the roles of their kids, and the kids are now the parents. Wives now become husbands, and husbands become wives, etc. The moderator then asks the same types of "Good Questions," but each group now has to respond as though they're in the opposite camp. They must try to see themselves from the eyes of the other. Looking at the other group is like looking in the mirror.

Generally that's the end of the moderator's work, because the dynamics usually care for themselves after that. The moderator must hold one rule above all: He or she must have the right to call time out on anything or anyone that begins to move toward the negative or derogatory, or that is lacking in respect. This must be absolutely understood. (Remember, Elijah draws hearts together!)

You'll wish to conclude with some good singing or something else geared to unity.

How It Has Worked:

This must be moderated well and have the mood set correctly. You can't do this just to fill time. The worst thing that could happen in this type of exercise is to allow it to deteriorate into a gripe session.

Sabbath Activity Thirty-eight

The Sabbath Crest

Theme and Rationale:

For more than a thousand years throughout Western Europe generations of people grew up with a very visual and ever present sense of identity. The children of the elite were raised under "the sign of the house of _____." The family crest was a marking to be honored and gave an anchor to a person's identity throughout life.

But most people lived as the base of support for the pyramid of society. The top had very little room. Those folks knew who they were by the herald or crest of their town or province.

People today seem to live in constant transition. Various popular personalities have believed that various symbols well represent life today. John Denver said it was credit cards (tomorrow stolen by plastic). Walter Cronkite said the symbol should be cellophane tape (impermanent patching). John Steinbeck said modern society is best understood by looking at a mobile home (no roots).

All these concepts are antithetical to terms like *tradition, legacy, heritage, continuity,* and *family.*

The art of the heraldic crest challenges our lack of heritage.

Minimum Time Required:

Not less than an hour.

Preparation and Materials:

Probably the best preparation would be to collect various books on, or pictures of, family crests to display during the time that your group is working on the project.

The Sabbath Crest

How To:

You'll want first to discuss our loss of the sense of legacy. Then determine if the herald crest is being created by individuals for their family or whether there will be a "competition" for a church or school crest.

1. Begin the exercise by selecting from the four basic shield shapes. Then determine its divisions. This is done by using "quartering" or "ordinaries," which are the stripes and bands.

2. "Charges" then are chosen. These could represent various values that are important to those who live under the crest. For Christianity there could be a cross, a lamb, a dove, etc.; for education there could be a book, a ruler, a lamp, a scroll, etc.; other symbols could represent skills, hobbies, trades, professions, home, character strengths, talents, or health.

3. Next the traditional "tinctures" (colors) are selected. Historically they've been black, purple, green, red, tan, and blue. Generally white has represented silver, and yellow has represented gold. It's best to have strong contrasts of dark on light and light on dark.

4. Some crests have helmets or crowns and a mantle of leaves around the shield or border.

5. The motto ribbon is draped along the bottom and provides a special opportunity to make a specific and focused statement of faith and values.

6. Historically there have been two taboos for shields: don't display letters or numbers and don't "quarter" the shield and then fill each zone with unrelated symbols. (Have two crosses and one scroll or a Bible and four trumpets rather than a Bible, a cross, a violin, and a quill pen.)

After the rough design and plan is decided upon, the participants will want to work toward making a final product that can be proudly kept. Any number of media could be utilized—pen and ink, sand painting (see activity 36 for description of this method), silhouette cut-outs, balsa wood, flour dough (see activity 33 for the recipe), or some other creative method.

How It Has Worked:

This is a rather new thought to me, and I'm looking forward to letting this bless some Sabbaths for me in the near future.

FSA-7

Sabbath Activity Thirty-nine

Bible May I?

Theme and Rationale:
Few enjoyable Bible games allow people of all stages of Bible knowledge to participate without fear. Usually those who have a greater grasp of Bible stories through the privilege of many years of Bible classes in church school blow away the "second class citizens" who weren't raised in the system.

As with anything that reveals the differences between classes, this may be satisfactory to the mainstream, but it can be just one more burden to bear for those who haven't had the privilege of Christian education. No minority needs one more threatening reminder of its status.

As we've seen, the true Elijah message unifies hearts and doesn't drive additional wedges among members. This Bible May I activity puts everyone older than 8 years on equal footing. Only walking biblical encyclopedias have any advantage, and there's even a way to put them on the same playing field as everyone else.

But still, it's not a game of chance.

Minimum Time Required:
A half hour or more.

Preparation and Materials:
The only preparation is an investment of time on the part of the game master or team that will assist if that person feels limited in ability to research and create the questions for the game. Creating this game is work, but it's worth it.

How To:
A good reservoir of 30 to 40 questions has to be created. These

Bible May I?

need to be statements or questions with three plausible answers for each. It's best not to lean toward absolutely insignificant trivia, because good trivia knowledge only makes a person a repository of useless knowledge, and people get bored with that. Here are some samples:

What does the name Bethlehem mean?
    Town of shepherds   House of bread   Valley of sheep

Whose name is an important prophecy?
    Methuselah   Noah   Enoch

Which Temple gate was the gate of pilgrims?
    Sheep Gate   Gate Beautiful   Eastern Gate

Which anti-Roman revolutionary was not alive during the days of Paul?
    Simon Bar Cocheba   Theudas   Judas of Galilee

These are good, challenging facts that would lead a person to want to know more and would enhance the Bible stories.

You line up all the participants shoulder to shoulder in a space where they can take steps forward. You first read the question so that they can individually determine what they will choose, and then you force them to decision. At the second reading each person is to take one step forward upon hearing the answer that he or she believes to be true. This forces each person to "take a stand" for his or her choice. (It goes like this, "If you believe the answer is Simon Bar Cocheba, take one step forward. If you believe the answer is Theudas, take one step forward. If you believe it is Judas of Galilee, step forward. Those of you who think it is Simon Bar Cocheba get to stay; the rest of you take one step back.")

Within just a very few questions, the line gets quite scattered, and it's fun to see who is progressing and who isn't getting off the starting line. You may have a set goal for "winning" and then start the game over again. Rarely will you have the same person win twice.

Winning for the vast majority of people will be almost blind luck. But the structure of the game and the knowledge offered in well-structured, well-planned questions create an entertaining yet educational atmosphere, even though it may not appear that way.

How It Has Worked:

I've used this game many times in a variety of forums. It has always worked, even with a line of 50 people.

PS: The other answers were House of bread, Methuselah, and Gate Beautiful.

Sabbath Activity Forty

The "What If?" Challenge

Theme and Rationale:

I'm particularly grateful that the Bible doesn't tell us absolutely every detail of every story. It's not unlike the difference between watching a story on TV or in a movie and hearing the same story dramatized on tape or radio. The movie is never as good as the book; it can't be. The creation of your imagination is much more fulfilling than the vision portrayed by some director.

If every facet of each Bible story were given, it would leave no room for us to incorporate it into our own individual experience. Your perception of Moses meets your needs, but probably wouldn't meet mine.

And it appears that God isn't at all troubled by this type of speculation. He establishes walls around the truth, and Scripture demands that you remain within those walls. It's not appropriate to speculate that Moses was born to Pharaoh's daughter and not Jochebed. But if you want to believe that Moses was left handed, then go ahead—just don't determine my sincerity by whether or not I accept your speculative arguments.

That's why doing the Bible "What If?" Challenge is fun. You may be right. I may be right. Or neither of us may be right. But we'll have our ideas stretched by each other's imagination, and we'll find ways to put flesh on the story skeleton given in Scripture.

Minimum Time Required:

At least an hour; usually this goes longer than you think because people begin to loosen up and really get into it.

Preparation and Materials:

All that's needed is an investment of time and thinking. You must prepare a list of Bible stories that you'll ask "What if?" about. This isn't as

The "What If?" Challenge

easy as it may seem. But once you start flowing in the track of that thinking, you'll find that they jump out at you, and the list will begin to swell.

How To:

First spend a little time explaining that everything that will be done is going to be only speculation. No participants will have a monopoly on the "truth" when they begin to think in those terms.

Next you'll break the group into workable teams. Usually five or six team members are good for this type of exercise. (Fewer than that number will often find one person dominating, and the size will also limit what participants are able to portray. More than that, and it becomes too easy for some participants to fade into the background. This is just simple group dynamic rules that experience proves almost universally true.)

Tell the groups that they'll all be given five minutes to create a mini-enactment based upon the assigned story. When the five minutes are up, they'll be expected to act out what they've speculated. Then give them their first assignment. It could be something like one of the following:

"What if . . .

> Judas had repented when Jesus washed his feet that night in the upper room?
> Moses had not run to Midian but stayed in Egypt to start an insurrection?
> all the disciples had decided to walk out to Jesus on the water?
> Nero had repented and been converted when Paul faced him in trial?
> the priests had accepted Jesus and led the people to proclaim Him king instead of crucify Him?
> Joseph had given in to Potiphar's wife?

You must stress that all this involves speculation. There are no right or wrong responses as long as there's no contradiction of the biblical data.

How It Has Worked:

This has worked really well with groups of teens and adults. I've done three or four in a row, but it must be kept moving. Lag time will kill an exercise like this. Don't force discussion. It will happen on its own, and that's when it's most effective.

Sabbath Activity Forty-one

The Lord's Prayer Hunt

Theme and Rationale:
Not every valuable activity requires the leader to do all the work. Sometimes it's best just to give people the parameters of expectations and let them create the activity. Good growth and challenge means that we aren't baby-sat every moment. There's a special joy in being given the skeleton of an assignment and being turned free to accomplish it.

Usually just being given creative freedom inspires sparks of creativity, and creativity compounds to greater creativity. The Lord's Prayer Hunt is such a challenge.

Minimum Time Required:
An hour and a half could be the minimum, but to avoid chaos this exercise demands a very specific set time for conclusion.

Preparation and Materials:
Merry Christmas from me! This one requires no preparatory work on your part! All that's necessary is simply to get the participants together, determine your time frame, and turn them loose.

How To:
It's best to start with some unifying activity. This gives a sense of beginning.

After the lead-in the participants are divided into teams of four to six people. Explain the assignment and the time limit in which they're to accomplish their task, and let them be off.

The assignment is simple. Each group is to break the Lord's Prayer into its individual phrases and then decide how they're going to portray each of the 11 phrases through collecting things in a scavenger hunt.

The Lord's Prayer Hunt

"Our Father which art in heaven,
"Hallowed be thy name.
"Thy kingdom come.
"Thy will be done in earth, as it is in heaven.
"Give us this day our daily bread.
"And forgive us our debts, as we forgive our debtors.
"And lead us not into temptation,
"But deliver us from evil:
"For thine is the kingdom,
"and the power,
"and the glory, for ever" (Matt. 6:9-13).

At the appointed time they're to bring back and show to the other groups what they've collected to portray each phrase.

The rules are also simple.
1. Nothing is to be purchased.
2. Nothing is to be cutesy or bordering on the sacrilegious.
3. Nothing is to be utilized without permission of the owner.
4. The participants must be able to demonstrate it to the group.

Don't give any more rules, because you don't want to stop any possibility of how they might create the fulfillment of the assignment.

When the appointed conclusion time arrives, let each team demonstrate what it's done.

How It Has Worked:

With any event like this you'll find that each group will come up with at least two or three things that are incredibly creative. People say to themselves, "Wow, why didn't we think of that?"

This is especially true with teens. It seems to be universally true that the "troublemakers," who often show no particular bent to spiritual things, blossom in things like this. They're given freedom to express themselves, and that's the opposite of why they often make trouble—they're itching for a forum to express themselves without the traditional expectations that they feel encumber their perception of religion.

PS: This can be adapted to be The Ten Commandments Hunt, or The Great Ten Parable Hunt, or The Seven Days of Creation Hunt, or . . .

Sabbath Activity Forty-two

The Language of Heaven

Theme and Rationale:
It's easy to understand why Isaiah and Paul felt that heaven would be more than anyone could even think or dream (Isa. 64:4 and 1 Cor. 2:9). After all, they were primitives, and they'd never even seen a television.

But aren't we the generation that has been blessed by the sensory explosions created by George Lucas and Industrial Light and Magic? Aren't we the ones who live on the edge of virtual reality? Hasn't *Star Trek* taught us that we could create hologram decks in which to experience artificially the images of our dreams? We are advanced. What is beyond us? "Professing themselves to be wise, they became fools" (Rom. 1:22).

Minimum Time Required:
About an hour.

Preparation and Materials:
The first part of this will take some advance time on your part. You must think of the five senses and how they could be challenged.

Three that I've tried required the following:

A musical tape of a selection not commonly known by most people. (I've used some of the concluding choral sections of "Vita Nostra," by Morricone, from the soundtrack of *The Mission*; Debussy's "Engulfed Cathedral," done on synthesizer by several artists, or the concluding portions of "What Wondrous Love," by Jeff Johnson. They are all challenging, little known, and difficult to describe.)

For taste challenge I've found some oriental crackers that aren't exactly sweet, but they have a saltiness that hides a touch of licorice. (Get it?) Or root beer mixed with orange soda tastes unusual.

For visual imaging I've draped shimmering cloth through a box with

The Language of Heaven

a Plexiglas tube extended diagonally and drapings of white shimmering ribbon with miscellaneous shapes. If you seal the box and provide only three different openings for a person to look into, you have to shine a flashlight on one end of the tube extending out of the box to provide light for the inside. It creates eerie images.

How To:

After you've worked to create at least three sensory challenges for the group, you start your event by doing some unity events.

Then have an assistant who will lead three or four of the group away from the rest of the people so that this little group can listen to the three- or four-minute passage of music. When they return, ask them to describe what they heard. It's fascinating to watch them struggle to verbalize the experience of the music.

Next bring up three or four others to partake in the tasting experience. After they've spent a few moments with the food or drink, ask them to describe what they've experienced.

Finally, let three or four look into your created visual experience, and have them struggle to describe what they saw there.

You conclude the first part by playing the music for the whole group, giving each a sample of the taste, and allowing a moment for all to look into the box.

The obvious result will be that all will better understand the difficulty in comprehending what their senses have experienced. Take them immediately to 1 Corinthians 2:9 and discuss the concept that heaven will exceed our wildest dreams.

If you wish to make this an even more creative experience, let them work in teams to create more sensory challenges. What else could be done to spotlight touch? taste? hearing? smell? sight? This could almost become a "competition" if your group has access to resources at that time.

The ultimate end would be to have the group describe 10 sensory things about heaven that they feel no one else has ever considered—for instance, reaching into the river of life to drink will bring fish that want to be petted! Or the water from the river of life will slip through your fingers and splatter . . . and each splash will produce a flower!

C. S. Lewis says that we'll be able to swim up waterfalls.

How It Has Worked:

It has been an eye-opener. Groups that I've done this with have indicated that this activity brought new vistas of thought regarding our limitations and what heaven could be. It sure challenges harps and clouds!

Sabbath Activity Forty-three

The Jerusalem Miniature

Theme and Rationale:
Those of us who have the privilege of living in Arizona don't have to face the cold, blustery Sabbaths of winter when a nice fire and a good indoor activity are called for. (If anything, we need those type of events in mid-August when it's 114 degrees outside!)

The Jerusalem Miniature is such an activity. It can be a blessing on a long, slow, relaxing Sabbath afternoon. A bit of good background music or story tapes, good friends, and a ton of toothpicks and peas . . .

Sometimes it doesn't get any better than this!

Minimum Time Required:
Who's in a hurry?

Preparation and Materials:
The amount of materials needed will depend on the size of the group you expect to participate.

This activity calls for three ingredients. You can provide two of them and set the atmosphere to have your participants bring the third.

You'll need to provide a lot of round toothpicks. By a lot, I mean boxes. You'll also need to prepare a big kettleful of soaked peas. (The soaking process isn't an exact science. Just put them in water and let them soak for six to nine hours. You can't oversoak them.)

Good background music or story tapes set a nice tone for the time that your group has together.

How To:
Let your group know that they're going to work on a joint participation project. They're to determine various things that they know were in

The Jerusalem Miniature

the city of Jerusalem during the days of Jesus. They may also create some things that they assume would have been in a city of the age.

Here's a partial listing:
- the Temple
- the assembly room of the Sanhedrin
- the house of the high priest
- the Fortress of Antonia (barracks of the Roman garrison)
- the king's palace
- Bethesda (the gate of five porches)
- a house and the upper room
- the city wall
- various shops, homes, public buildings

After they've determined how much of the city they wish to create, let them divide up the structures so that each person is working on something. The larger buildings could be up to 18 inches tall and wide. Lesser structures, such as homes or shops, should be proportionately smaller—a market in a bazaar could be perhaps six inches long and four inches wide.

It's difficult to have more than one person work on the same building. Each person should have his or her own assigned construction project.

The structures are created in a style like the old Tinker Toys building sets. A toothpick is stuck into a pea and then another toothpick maybe comes out of the pea at a 90-degree angle to the right or left, up or down. Perhaps another toothpick comes out the other side in a continuation of the line—whatever combination is needed to create the angles necessary for your building.

Towers and minarets can be designed to fit into the wall. Gates can be left open. Roof lines can be uniquely created for each structure.

The only limit to this project is the imagination of those who take part.

How It Has Worked:

I've not done this myself, but I have a very creative friend who utilizes the same style of creations for his students, and it's really challenging.

The nonthreatening nature of this type of exercise is good for a large variety of people. The artistically gifted can enjoy it, and the rest of us can take part without being intimidated.

Your finished product could very well be something the group could be proud of. Then what do you do with it?

Sabbath Activity Forty-four

The Adam and Eve Walk

Theme and Rationale:

Mark Twain took issue with a lot of his perceptions of traditional religious understandings. Some of what he said is worth considering, because it challenges certain sacred cows in mainstream Christian thought. His *Letters From the Earth* raised many of the same issues that C. S. Lewis did in *The Screwtape Letters*, but long before Lewis knew how to write the alphabet.

It's sad that old Clemens seems to have died a struggling, unfulfilled man.

Some of the interesting and challenging pieces from Twain's imagination are the "diaries" of Adam and Eve. (Some may see it as a bit sacrilegious. I guess I consider the source and find it a little refreshing. There goes my credibility with some! I'm sorry that I'm not as sorry as I should be.)

Twain speculates that Adam and Eve had a lot to learn. Their minds were blank slates, so they had to learn by experience because they had no experiences to use as reference points. Hence Eve sees meteorites and decides she wants to stare at the sky every night so that she'll "remember what they looked like after they have all melted out of the darkness."

And how would you name an aardvark? How would you describe it if you hadn't yet named a cat or a pig or the color brown? And why aren't butterflies called flutter-bys? And why aren't anteaters called eat-anters, as Johnny Hart says in the comic strip *B.C.*?

Do you get the point?

Minimum Time Required:

Probably more than an hour.

The Adam and Eve Walk

Preparation and Materials:

Good news: you don't have to do anything! You may wish to get a copy of the diaries and read some of the portions that you feel would assist in giving inspiration for the assignment. (Meredith Baxter-Birney and David Birney turned these into a two-person play for PBS around 1990, but I saw only small portions of it about five years ago and sense that using it in any format may set you up for criticism from some who think it really is sacrilegious.)

How To:

Explain that this really is a lot like a game. The group is going to discover the world. Let them consider how difficult it is to describe things when you don't have names for colors or animals or body parts.

Let them break into teams of three to four people (maybe up to six or so if you have a large group). Tell them that they have 20 minutes to discover and plan how they're going to describe what they found. They must discover at least five items: One is nonliving; one is living material, but not from the animal kingdom; one has to be from the animal kingdom near their location; one has to be from the animal kingdom, but not near that location; and the last one can be anything they choose.

Then turn them loose to discover the world.

After 20 minutes let the teams stand up and describe what they have discovered. They have to remember that they don't have reference points that are normal to all of us. What is the sky anyway? What is yellow like? How do you imitate the noise a wind makes in leaves?

It's really fun to see how creative they can be in describing and acting out the items they've selected on their imaginary search.

There could be a prize awarded to the team that provides the greatest creativity and joy to the group.

How It Has Worked:

I always fear that exercises like this are going to bomb, but they never do. It seems that people rise to the challenge when they're released to creativity. This type of event is really unifying and enjoyable.

Sabbath Activity Forty-five

The Christmas Jewels

Theme and Rationale:
Many Adventists struggle with the issues of how to relate to the trappings of Christmas. Some are very vocal about the pagan origins of most of the season, and they regard it a terrible compromise to the faith to participate in any of the Christmas spirit.

It isn't my place to doubt their sincerity, but the emotion with which so many of them present their views is less than attractive. Angry prophets are impressive but awfully hard to want to spend much time around.

I personally feel that I'm not any more responsible for what a Christmas tree may have meant centuries ago than I am for the failure of the church in 1888. Despite the corporate guilt that some would have me carry, I wasn't even born yet.

This exercise can be used during the Christmas season, and it's usually much less offensive to those who have reservations than most things we may do.

Minimum Time Required:
About an hour.

Preparation and Materials:
You'll need to prepare two sets of items. First, purchase a good number of cheap, satin-thread-wound Christmas balls. (You'll often find them at surplus warehouses or bargain stores.) For this exercise white is the color of preference. You'll also need an ink pad and an assortment of various colors of ribbon.

Second, get a nice number of the cheapest regular glass-type Christmas balls you can find. Also purchase some sand. The color of the balls is of no regard here, but the sand should be grays and browns and

The Christmas Jewels

tans and perhaps one nice turquoise or lavender. You'll also need some cans of spray glue (available at any craft store) and some plastic straws, chop sticks, pencils, or something like that. Some little margarine tubs will fill out the materials necessary for your second set of items.

How To:
This activity could use a good background of music or story tapes.

The white thread-wound balls are for small children. Have someone assist them in tying bows or making streamers from the ribbon that can be connected to hang from the top of the balls. The ink pads are for the children to personalize the ball with their thumbprint. This way they represent themselves as "jewels" for Jesus' crown. (Didn't the old song say, "Little children, little children who love their Redeemer, are the jewels, precious jewels"?)

The glass balls and sand are for older children up to the age of 104. First pull out the little ring and crown that the hook connects to. Then soak the balls in water for a minute or two. This allows you to peel off the paint from the surface. (The spray glue will bubble on the surface if you don't remove the paint layer.)

Gently dry the balls and then put a pencil or straw or something in the hole and shoot a light layer of spray glue onto the balls and sprinkle one color of sand all over as the base coat.

After you've given the balls a moment to dry, spray another light layer of glue and then roll the balls in a margarine tub filled with another color of sand. Don't cover the whole ball. Perhaps just 70 percent from the bottom up, not necessarily at an even angle as the ball would hang.

After a few minutes of drying, you could add another contrasting color at a different angle, covering 30 percent or so.

When the balls are completed, the older folks have also created a unique gift to decorate the tree that the world associates with a symbol Christ's birth.

How It Has Worked:
By focusing on making gifts that represent "me" for Jesus, a lot of the potential criticism of Christmas trappings has been defused. (Giving the results to a nursing home might help even more.) In fact, equating my little symbols to my place in the crown of Christ is a rather joyous thought!

Sabbath Activity Forty-six

Living Psalms

Theme and Rationale:
We wonder what the psalms originally sounded like when sung. What was the texture and timbre of the music? Were there solo parts? Was there rhythm as we know it for the verse patterns? Did they repeat a chorus? Were they ever transformed into a speech choir style?

Why should we be limited in our use of these Scripture gems?

Minimum Time Required:
Probably an hour.

Preparation and Materials:
It would help if you provided a copy of the various psalms you choose, taken from a translation that is *not* the King James. I prefer the Jewish Publication Society translation called the *Tanakh* for all Old Testament issues. (But you'd expect that from someone whose graduate stuff was done exclusively in Jewish studies, wouldn't you?)

How To:
Pick a list of some of the particularly colorful psalms for your group to use as the foundation for their presentations. Here are some of my own personal preferences for this type of experience: Psalms 7, 8, 11, 13, 19, 47, 61, 87, 91, 93, 114, 122, 125, 126, 133, 137, 147.

Once you've divided the participants into groups of six or so, give them one of the selected psalms and tell them that they'll have 10 minutes to make the psalm live.

There are very few restrictions. Obviously the end product should not be cheap, cutesy, or sacrilegious. Other than that, the only requirement is that every member of the team should have some role in the presenta-

Living Psalms

tion. Then dismiss them to some solitude so that they can work on their creations without distractions.

Be particular about your time frame. Don't allow lingering at the end, because what is catching-up time to one group is absolutely dead time to another. Nothing destroys the potential of enthusiasm as easily as dead time when you're ready to go.

Free Hint—No Extra Charge: *This is always a rule in working with groups. Just as it's imperative to have them feel that they didn't quite have enough time (so that they feel "We must have really been into this . . ."), so also you must not allow dead time. Be strict about time assignments. That will give the sense that productive work is being done.*

Timeliness lends more than just credibility to the assignment.

When the assigned time is completed, let the various groups share their presentations. You'll be amazed at how they've breathed life into the psalms.

How It Has Worked:

This has been a great activity. I've seen groups make the psalm into a song, play, skit, parable, game, and even rap that was honest and impressive. I've seen them complete the first group of assigned psalms and ask, "Can we do one more?"

I usually don't let them. The first cycle seems to be the creative one, and any that come afterward usually fall into an adaptation of what they've seen others do. I'd rather have the creative moment linger. I feel it's more productive.

Sabbath Activity Forty-seven

Muddy Fingernails

Theme and Rationale:

To "anthropomorphize" is to project human characteristics upon things that aren't human. Some examples of that would include, for example, "Under the watchful eye of the setting sun," "The strong arms of the oak," and "The wind spoke assurance."

Theologians see this as problematic when we discuss God. The Word says that we're created in His image, but how Godlike are we really? And how much like us is God?

This activity provides a double challenge that can remind us of what Genesis proclaims the creation was really like. It's fun to envision God with muddy fingernails.

Minimum Time Required:

It would be best to plan for at least two hours.

Preparation and Materials:

You'll need to provide for both facets of the activity.

The first stage is to find a potter who actively plies the craft. You'll predispose this to real success if you can find a person who exudes some vibrancy, is pleasant to be around, understands (and can be supportive of) what you're doing this for, and portrays a Christian influence.

The second stage of the activity requires you to provide enough modeling clay for each participant to have a glob about the size of a softball or grapefruit. You'll also need to provide a location that gives worktable space for your group, newspapers to keep the place clean, some containers for water, etc.

Good music enhances the background for part two of the activity.

Muddy Fingernails

How To:

First let the group observe the potter sitting at the wheel. If you've found the right person, he or she will not only exhibit skill, but will describe the process and interact with the participants in a fascinating way.

Those who have never seen this craft will be mesmerized. Before their eyes the dead lump of clay will come alive in the skillful hands of the potter. A gifted potter almost makes the clay sing as it's transformed into a vessel of usefulness.

The obvious conclusion for the first stage is to consider the concepts presented in Isaiah 64:8, Jeremiah 18:4-6, Lamentations 4:2, and Romans 9:21.

For the second stage let the group consider for a moment the implications of Genesis 2:7. It's amazing to grasp a picture of God with dirty hands.

Then give your participants the privilege of trying to create just a portion of a human being. I'd recommend an ear. It's a whale of a lot harder than it might seem to anyone who has never tried.

With good music in the background and a pleasant atmosphere, your group will gain incredible insights into the fact that God did not remain removed from His creative acts. The Bible says our God was intimately involved with His children from the beginning.

Shaping an ear from clay teaches two things: (1) the act of genius in the Creation is amazing, and (2) I could love a God with muddy fingernails.

How It Has Worked:

I've seen a really skilled potter hold a large group in rapt attention for about 20 minutes. His interaction was so pleasant and the "sermon" presented was so far removed from being "preachy" that even the most uninvolved and least committed were drawn to the message.

The ear creation has been a delightful way to catch the lessons too.

PS: I'll never forget the unified groan when the potter concluded his portion by stopping the wheel and suddenly crushing the beautiful vessel he'd just created. That was a provocative lesson too.

48

Sabbath Activity Forty-eight

The Family Courtroom

Theme and Rationale:
Very few of us are so incorrigible that we set out specifically to offend. Somehow it just seems to happen from our weakness. That's what carnality is all about.

The Family Courtroom activity provides a forum to remind us that all of us are working from a frame of reference that's been distorted by sin. Parents need that reminder, and so do their kids.

Minimum Time Required:
Probably an hour or so.

Preparation and Materials:
You get away fairly easily this time. All that's needed to make this event happen is to recruit in advance three bright, capable, energetic people to serve as "prosecutor," "defense attorney," and "judge" for the courtroom.

Once you've found the right people, you'll need to spend some time brainstorming about issues to be addressed during the trial phase of the activity. They'll need to come up with a list of generic "charges" that many kids might commonly level against their parents in a typical home. The charges could be related to rules, privileges, expectations, etc. The goal is to open up, in a friendly way, conflict points that are common in most families.

How To:
At the appointed hour your group is waiting in the "courtroom." Explain that you'll need all parents to sit on the right side (facing the judge). All the nonparents are to sit on the left.

When they've situated themselves appropriately, explain that they've

The Family Courtroom

now reversed roles. The right side is the side of the prosecution. The older ones are now going to make accusation against the younger participants for decisions they've made in their parenting.

(This is very important. The role reversal creates an atmosphere that will remain light, because it isn't based on the normal relational interactions. It would be difficult for this to deteriorate into a situation in which everyone falls into normal ruts, because no one is in his or her normal role. If you don't reverse roles, you're asking for trouble.)

The nonparents then are told that their "children" have come to lay charges against them for their failures and unfairness in parenting. The judge randomly selects one of the "parents" (who could be a 15-year-old) and shares what the charges against him or her are. From that point on the "lawyers" and "judge" carry the ball. The "prosecutor" may call any "witnesses" he or she chooses to try to substantiate the claims, and the "defense attorney" may counter with questions and witnesses of his or her own.

When it seems that sufficient benefit has been derived from the first trial, let the "judge" render a verdict and then move on to another mini-trial. Some other "parent" will be accused of something else, such as "unreasonable cruelty by limiting TV on school nights" or "unjust rules regarding who my friends are and what I can do with them."

When you sense that you've derived about all the benefit you can from the first portion of the exercise move on to stage two. (Don't linger over it if the horse is dead!) Tell the real nonparents that they won't be allowed to speak at all while the parents share something interesting. (If they're allowed to interject comments, it can destroy the positive mood very quickly.)

Tell the real parents that the Bible admonishes that we aren't to "provoke" our "children to wrath" (Eph. 6:4). Tell them they have only a few minutes to come up with every way that their own parents provoked them to wrath when they were growing up. This is always an eye-opener. You'll get all the statements that their own children would say: "Why can't you be like . . ." "When I was a kid . . ." "Because I said so . . ." "Didn't accept my friends . . ." "Punished me unfairly . . ." "Didn't believe me . . ."

Their own kids will be amazed, and the parents will learn a lesson.

How It Has Worked:

With the right people guiding this, it truly can be a unifying experience for families. It helps kids see the dilemmas of parenting and momentarily reminds parents what it's like to be a kid.

Sabbath Activity Forty-nine

Parables Now

Theme and Rationale:

"Familiarity breeds contempt," or so they say. In theory that's not supposed to be true. Familiarity is supposed to bring intimacy. But it's true that human nature tends to allow the familiar to become ordinary. It's said that if the stars came out only once every thousand years, we'd call it a miracle.

This sad truth spills over into our awe for Christ's words. What He taught was absolutely revolutionary, and His proclamations were the most freeing statements the world has ever heard.

But we tend to sleep when we hear the words "A sower went forth to sow . . ."

The Parables Now activity gives the opportunity to allow the words to come back to life with a new power.

Minimum Time Required:

Could be an hour, could take more if the group really gets into it.

Preparation and Materials:

The best way to prepare for this exercise is to use a harmony of the Gospels to make a list of all the parables Jesus told—even the lesser known ones.

Prepare a comprehensive list of them along with their Scripture references. Luke has most of them, but it helps to have all references so that the various nuances available in each of the Gospels can be seen.

Put a single parable (with references) on a note card.

Provide a variety of Bibles so that the participants can look up the parables.

Parables Now

How To:

Begin the activity by doing some unifying activity like singing or another mixer-type event. Then when you sense that the group is warmed up and ready to get to work, have them break into teams of four to six people.

After they've formed workable teams, put all the parable note cards into a box or a paper bag. Mix the cards, and then pull them out one at a time until each team has a parable assignment.

Tell the participants that they have 10 minutes to prepare to bring the parable to life. Other than avoiding sacrilege and making sure that all members of the team take part in the presentation, there are no rules.

Don't even give a hint as to what may be done. As soon as you make any recommendation, it psychologically makes a box that seems to stifle creativity. Very few people are geared to thinking to go beyond the assignment, even if it's only an implied assignment.

As always, be acutely sensitive to the time limit you've set for preparation. If people understand that delays or grace periods will not be given, they're more efficient. It also guarantees that you'll avoid that great energy killer, lag time.

When the time has elapsed, let the groups randomly make their presentations. You'll be amazed at the ingenuity that some display in showing insights into the old, familiar stories.

If the first round has gone well, you may go through the exercise again. Urge them to portray their second parable in a different manner than they did the first one.

When they return, let them show their stuff in a reverse order from how they did the first set.

How It Has Worked:

This has been a good exercise to challenge people to see the famous old stories in a new light. I'm always amazed at how this type of event brings out unforeseen creativity and usually causes those who normally sit on the fringe to become actively involved.

Sabbath Activity Fifty

The Ministry Cycle

Theme and Rationale:

Many of us decry church "politics." We get frustrated when it looks as though sister churches are in competition. We'd like to believe that we're all in the business of building up the kingdom, but God has put the treasure into earthen vessels, and those vessels still have some flaws in the clay.

Competition between churches comes from normal human concerns: security, sense of identity, the desire to look good, and the mundane issue of who will pay the bills.

In the heavenly kingdom there will be no human pettiness, but as long as we're here on this earth we'll have to deal with the potential of humans who tend to mark their territory.

The Ministry Cycle activity requires two things: (1) three churches within 15 minutes' drive of one another, and (2) leadership of three churches who would be willing to risk their normal territorialism for an opportunity to participate in a wonderful experience.

Minimum Time Required:

The morning worship service, and it probably will have to be extended.

Preparation and Materials:

Bring together the leadership of three churches and plan the event together. Each church will provide one brief children's story, one special music, a short devotional, and a person capable of leading out in singing.

Once the ministry teams have been decided upon, a three-part theme for the whole service should be determined. (Concepts about the Trinity would seem to be a natural or perhaps something about Peter, James, and John or about faith, hope, and charity.)

The Ministry Cycle

The only thing left to do is to negotiate the logistics and timing for the activity.

How To:

Let each ministry team begin in their home church. They'll have 15 minutes for their portion. Then the assigned song leader in each church will keep the service moving until the arrival of the next ministry team.

Team A will move on to church B, as team B moves on to church C, etc.

It may be that some of the filler time could be utilized in ways other than singing. An attractive slide program or multimedia presentation could provide a pleasant change if the church is capable of providing something attractive and challenging.

At the conclusion of the three presentations one of several wrap-ups could be utilized. There could be a tape available of several members of each church giving public testimonies of gratitude for their church family, which could then be played the next Sabbath for the other churches. The head elder of each church could end with a prayer on the tape, specifically asking for God's blessing on the sister churches.

Another ending might be a centrally located joint potluck fellowship meal in a nearby park or school gymnasium.

How It Has Worked:

I've never tried this activity. I don't know why. It seems to have promise and could turn out to be a great event.

Of course, if you live in Smallville and the nearest sister church is 43 miles away, this probably would need serious adaptation. I guess you'd have to be very creative to get it done then.

Sabbath Activity Fifty-one

Sabbath Monuments

Theme and Rationale:

No one knows as well as the Lord that we are all frail and dust. The Word records that Jesus "knew what was in man" (John 2:25). He knows we tend to forget. The old hymn says, "Prone to wander, Lord, I feel it, prone to leave the God I love."

Should we be surprised, then, that God admonished His people to establish methods for remembering? Deuteronomy 6 addresses the concept of remembering.

Sabbath Monuments is a particularly meaningful way to conclude some special event or holiday season.

Minimum Time Required:

Probably an hour or so.

Preparation and Materials:

This exercise takes very little preparation. All you need is a location with some nice stones or boulders and permission to take 12 of them.

How To:

As part of some special event or activity that you wish to commemorate as being particularly blessed, you'll dedicate the ending of the Sabbath with the establishment of the Sabbath memorial.

This could be used for
the weekend of a wedding,
the conclusion of a retreat or camp out,
to end a Week of Prayer,
the final act at a large family reunion,
the Sabbath following a funeral,

Sabbath Monuments

an act of farewell to someone moving far away

The uses of this are nearly limitless.

At the predetermined time get all participants out where the boulders and stones are. Review briefly the experience of the Israelites coming up out of the Jordan, recorded in Joshua 4. They'd just left the remnants of Egypt behind and now stood in the Promised Land. There they left a simple monument commemorating God's faithfulness and generosity.

Break your group into teams so that 12 stones can be carried equitably. It would be best if there was a pickup available to transport the stones to the location where the monument will be established.

Let the individuals or teams then go find a stone that appeals to them and bring it to the truck. Then let everyone go to the site determined for the monument.

Upon arrival it would be appropriate to have a prayer to ask the Lord's blessing upon the act of memorial. One at a time the stones are put into a pile. As with the established altars of Exodus 20, there should be no shaping or design. Just let nature do its work.

As each stone is set in place at least one person should make a pronouncement taken from the Passover Seder. Let the statement take the form of "It would have been enough that God would have _____, but instead He showed His generosity by _____."

Here are some samples: "It would have been enough that God gave me a precious bride, but instead He also gave me a new precious family." "It would have been enough that God allowed me to go to a Christian school, but instead He gave me this great Week of Prayer." "It would have been enough that God forgave me of my sins, but instead He allowed me to be baptized into a church I love." "It would have been enough that God gave me children, but instead He gave me the opportunity to live to see them become special men and women."

Do you see the beauty of it? They'll never pass those stones without remembering that experience.

How It Has Worked:

I know a place where those stones still stand after six years. I remember the day we placed them there. I know a lot of people who do too.

Sabbath Activity Fifty-two

Kingdom Reunions

Theme and Rationale:
I don't know how many "calls" have been given in which I've been asked to make an appointment for the first Sabbath in heaven. I honestly can't remember at this point if I'm to go to the west side of the river of life directly under the tree of life or if I'm to go to the east side of God's throne. (Maybe that's one reason for individual guardian angels. My angel will have to keep me on time at the various reunions that I've committed myself to throughout the years.)

But the whole concept of kingdom reunions raises a lot of special issues. If we truly believe that we'll know and be known by each other then, we're going to witness some remarkable meetings in that place. After all, what's it like to warm up an old joke after 3,000 years?

Minimum Time Required:
At least an hour; could end up to be more, maybe long after you officially end it. That's a neat thought, isn't it?

Preparation and Materials:
Spend some time meditating on Bible friends, couples, brothers, and families. As you think of them, write them on a sheet of paper. After coming up with a reasonable slate of names, put them into appropriate columns under the headings of Couples, Friends, Parents and Children, and Siblings.

Remember, you're considering those whom we may assume died in the good hope of the promise. Though it might be fun to see Moses confront Pharaoh again or watch Paul tell Nero, "I told you so," it isn't going to happen. Stick with those you believe have their names written in the Lamb's book of life. You'll have more than enough once you start.

Kingdom Reunions

Then get a chalkboard, poster board, or something on which you can write the four category headings in a way that all your participants will be able to see them. Leave the spaces blank, because the group will fill them in. Your list is just to assist them if they forget some good ones.

How To:

After utilizing some method of drawing the group to a beginning (singing or a game), turn their attention to the categories. Ask them to begin calling out names of people in the Bible who died looking forward to the day when they'd be reunited again.

Set a limit of five or six for any one category. Then as the slate is filled out, explain that you're going to speculate what that experience will be like.

Can you imagine what it will be like for Adam and Eve to embrace again? (And what will it make us feel like?) What stories will David have to tell Jonathan? What of Joseph and Mary? How about James and John? Peter and Andrew? What is John the Baptist going to tell old Zacharias and Elisabeth?

Break your group into teams of four or five and let them go through a mock draft to pick three sets of names that they're going to deal with. (Much like picking players for dodge ball at recess. One team gets to select names and then the next until you get to the last team, which gets to select two and reverse the order back to the first team.)

Then your teams huddle for three minutes. During that time they're to "flesh out" the imagined reunion. Where will it be held? Who will be the one to seek out the other? What will be asked? Who will say what? If someone was to bring a gift to the reunion, what would he or she bring? What apologies, amends, and explanations would have to be made? What will they do after they've had their initial meeting?

When the three minutes are finished, let each team share what they've speculated. Then have them huddle again to go through the same process for the other two sets of names they've chosen.

How It Has Worked:

Every activity that creates good imagination about the kingdom is positive. This exercise focuses us on the fact that someday we're going to move from this aberrant existence into living in the "real" universe. People feel good about speculating like this.

PS: I really do yearn to see Adam and Eve embrace.

Happy Sabbath!

Devotionals Just for Teens

**Peace Like a Spider
and Other Devotions for Teens**
Karl Haffner explores some of the Bible's best tips for helping teens succeed in their relationships, spiritual life, school, and on the job. Paper, 119 pages. US$7.95, Cdn$10.75.

**The Great Tennis Shoe Dilemma
and Other Devotions for Teens**
Gary B. Swanson helps teens grasp the scope of God's love and explores what it means to live as a Christian. Religious terms they've heard all their lives, such as *grace, salvation,* and *faith,* suddenly burst with new meaning. Paper, 112 pages. US$7.95, Cdn$10.75.

Available at all ABC Christian bookstores **(1-800-765-6955)** and other Christian bookstores. Prices and availability subject to change. Add GST in Canada.